Chilli Blooms

BY ANITA BHAGAT

Best Wishes

Anita Bhagat

First published in London, November 2013

by Liquid Bubble Media Ltd.

Text and photography copyright © Anita Bhagat

Edited by: Rashmi Madan

Design: Victoria Ireland

Cover Design: Trisha Bhagat

Photography: Jagu Hindocha

ISBN: 978-0-9927700-0-6

The decision to write this book came from the moment I began to tidy up the multitude of hand-written recipes I had floating all over the house. There were scribbles on old till receipts, notes on top of newspaper cuttings – not to mention the numerous ink-soaked napkins in my kitchen drawers. Grouped together, they marked my life as a wife and mother to my three children. Every recipe tells a story.

And so I began the painstaking task of typing up each and every one, archiving them in colour co-ordinated files. Unfortunately, I had typed them up in jargon that only I could understand! At around this time my daughters, who were both living abroad, would phone me every so often wanting a recipe or asking how I cooked their favourite dishes. So, once again, I found myself re-working those same bitty recipes in a more orderly fashion – thus sparking the desire to publish a cookbook for my children and future generations.

This is no ordinary recipe book, however. Each dish is the result of everything that I have learned or been taught over the years from family and friends. Many of the techniques used are unique to those of my mother and mother-in-law – passed down to them from their mothers, too. Being born a Punjabi and married to a Gujarati, I continue to have the best of both cuisines, and my cooking is an amazing fusion of the two distinct styles. I hope they will work just as beautifully for you.

Delight in food is delight in life.

Happy cooking.

Contents

Spice list

WHOLE URAD DAL

WASHED MOONG

RED KIDNEY BEANS

CHANNA

TOOR DAL

WHOLE MOONG

SPLIT CHANNA DAL

CURRY LEAVES

SESAME SEEDS

CRUSHED FENUGREEK SEEDS

CORIANDER POWDER

CITRIC ACID POWDER

CUMIN SEEDS

FENUGREEK SEEDS

RED CHILLI POWDER

WHITE CHILLI POWDER

COOKING WITH INDIAN SPICES MAY SEEM LIKE A TRICKY FEAT, BUT YOU'LL BECOME A MASTER CHEF IN NO TIME ONCE YOU'RE FAMILIAR WITH THESE ESSENTIAL INGREDIENTS

SPLIT MOONG

POMEGRANATE SEEDS

CORINADER SEEDS

STAR ANISE

WASHED URAD DAL

WHOLE NUTMEG

CINNAMON STICKS

CLOVES

ASAFOETIDA POWDER

SANCHORO (PAPAD KHAR)

CARDAMOM PODS

WHOLE MUSTARD SEEDS

DRY RED CHILLIES

GARAM MASALA

TURMERIC POWDER

CAROM SEEDS

Chef's tip

Store your spices in airtight containers in a cool, dark place – that way they'll keep their flavour (and punch) intact.

It's fun to get together
and have something good to
eat at least once a day. That's
what human life is all about
– enjoying things

JULIA CHILD

APPETISERS
& SNACKS

· · · · · · · · · · · · ·

Khichi

THESE SPICED AND STEAMED DUMPLINGS ARE TRADITIONALLY EATEN WITH A DRIZZLE OF OIL. GREAT FOR VEGETARIANS, TOO

Preparation time: 15 minutes
Cooking time: 30 minutes
Serves 6-8

You will need:

◇ *Water for boiling*
◇ *1 tbsp sanchoro (papad khar)*
◇ *2 tsp cumin seeds*
◇ *1 tbsp salt*
◇ *2 tsp carom seeds*
◇ *2 tsp fresh crushed green chillies*
◇ *2 cups rice flour*
◇ *Sesame seeds to garnish*
◇ *Cooking oil*
◇ *2 tsp fresh crushed garlic*

Method

1 Take ¼ cup of water, add the sanchoro and bring to boil. Leave aside.

2 Boil 2 cups of water in a large pot, add the cumin seeds, salt, carom seeds, chillies. Mix, then sieve the boiled sanchoro water into the large pot.

3 Add the 2 cups of rice flour, slowly mixing and stirring all the time until the mixture starts to stiffen.

4 Take off the heat and mix until it is soft. Make small flat circle shapes, make a hole in the middle (so that they look like doughnuts) and steam these for 30-40 minutes. When cooked, you will see the colour change slightly and they will be soft. Remove from the steamer and cut into small pieces.

5 Sprinkle over the sesame seeds and serve with a few drops of garlic oil (combine the cooking oil and fresh crushed garlic together).

6 This dish must be served hot. If it's cold, sprinkle with some water and microwave for 1 minute.

Bhajia/pakora

COMMONLY MADE WITH POTATOES AND ONIONS, OTHER VEGETABLES
SUCH AS AUBERGINES AND PEPPERS CAN ALSO BE USED

Preparation time: 10 minutes
Cooking time: 15 minutes
Serves 8-10

You will need:

◇ *1 cup gram flour*
◇ *3 tbsp warm water*
◇ *1 tsp salt*
◇ *1 tsp fresh crushed green chillies*
◇ *1 tsp red chilli powder*
◇ *½ tsp fresh crushed garlic*
◇ *½ tsp bicarbonate of soda*
◇ *1 potato peeled and sliced in circles*
◇ *1 onion sliced in circles*
◇ *Cooking oil to fry*

For the spinach bhajia:

◇ *2 cups finely chopped spinach instead
of the onions and potatoes. Remaining
ingredients are the same*

Method

1 Mix the gram flour with warm water and add salt, chililes, garlic and bicarbonate of soda.

2 Continue to mix to a fairly thick consistency, dip in the cut vegetables a few at a time and deep fry on a medium heat until the bhajias are golden brown.

3 Drain on paper towel. Serve hot with tomato ketchup or coriander chutney.

Method for spinach bhajia

1 Make the gram flour batter as above and add the spinach. Mix well.

2 Now place 1 tbsp of this batter in hot oil and deep fry on a medium heat until golden brown.

3 Place on some kitchen paper to remove any excess oil. Serve hot with coriander chutney.

Vegetable soup

MY MOTHER-IN-LAW'S FAMOUS SOUP! ALL GENERATIONS BEGGED HER TO COOK THIS DURING THE WINTER MONTHS. IT'S TASTY, WHOLESOME AND FULL OF GOODNESS

Preparation time: 10 minutes
Cooking time: 15 minutes
Serves 4

You will need:

◇ 2 beetroots
◇ 2 carrots
◇ 1 large potato
◇ 2 sticks celery
◇ 2 turnips
◇ 1 cup water
◇ 1 tbsp cooking oil
◇ 1 tsp fresh crushed garlic
◇ 1 tbsp butter
◇ Salt to taste
◇ Red chilli powder (optional)
◇ Freshly chopped coriander to garnish

Method

1 Wash and dice all the veg into small cubes.

2 Boil the vegetable cubes in a pressure cooker with 1 tsp salt and 1 cup water for 10-15 minutes.

3 Mash the vegetables to a thick consistency.

4 In another pot, heat the oil, add the garlic, mashed vegetables and the butter. Bring to boil and add salt and chilli powder to taste.

5 Garnish with coriander and serve hot.

Aloo poha

POTATO WITH POHA (FLATTENED RICE) BRINGS DELICIOUS TASTES OF SWEETNESS, SOURNESS, SOFTNESS AND CRUNCHINESS

Preparation time: 10 minutes
Cooking time: 10 minutes
Serves 4

You will need:

◇ 1 cup poha
◇ 2-3 potatoes washed and diced
◇ 2 tbsp cooking oil
◇ ½ tsp mustard seeds
◇ 1 tsp fresh crushed garlic
◇ 4-5 curry leaves
◇ 1 tsp fresh crushed green chillies
◇ Salt to taste
◇ 1 onion diced
◇ A pinch of turmeric powder
◇ 2 tbsp lemon juice
◇ Freshly chopped coriander to garnish

Method

1 Wash the poha in warm water, soak for 10 minutes, drain and keep aside. Do not soak it for longer than 10 minutes as it becomes soggy.

2 Blanche the diced potatoes in hot boiling water so that they are semi-cooked.

3 Heat the oil in a frying pan and add the mustard seeds. When the seeds start to pop add the garlic, the curry leaves and the potatoes. Add salt, green chillies, diced onion and turmeric. Stir and cook until the potatoes are soft.

4 Add the poha and the lemon juice, stir well. Cover and simmer for 5 minutes.

5 Serve hot garnished with chopped coriander.

Chef's tip

To add more flavour, the vadas may be topped with mint leaves instead of coriander and chilli powder.

Dahi vada or dahi bhalla

A POPULAR NORTH INDIAN STREET FOOD FARE. ABSOLUTELY YUMMY ON A HOT DAY AS A GREAT STARTER TO COOL THINGS DOWN

Preparation time: Soak overnight
Cooking time: 30 minutes
Serves 8

You will need:

◇ *1 cup urad dahl (white split urad)*
◇ *1 tsp salt*
◇ *1 tsp fresh crushed ginger*
◇ *Cooking oil to fry*

For the yoghurt:

◇ *1 tsp cooking oil*
◇ *A pinch of mustard seeds*
◇ *A few curry leaves*
◇ *2 cups plain yoghurt*
◇ *½ cup water*
◇ *1 tsp salt*
◇ *½ tsp red chilli powder*
◇ *2 tbsp cumin seeds*
◇ *Freshly chopped coriander to garnish*

Method

1 Prepare the vada by soaking the urad dahl in water overnight.

2 The following day, grind it in a blender with the salt and ginger to a thick consistency. You may need to add water to achieve soft balls.

3 Take 1 tsp of the mixture and pat it with your fingers so it forms a small circle. Deep fry these on a medium heat until light brown.

4 Remove from oil, drain on a paper towel and allow to cool. Keep these to one side. They can be frozen and stored for later use.

Method for the yoghurt

1 Heat the oil, add mustard seeds and curry leaves. When cool add this to the yoghurt.

2 Add ½ cup water, chillii and salt to taste.

3 Now, return to the vada and soak them in hot water.

4 Take each vada, flatten between palms to squeeze excess water out. Lay them flat in a dish and pour the yoghurt mixture over it.

5 Roast the cumin seeds until dark brown in colour and grind them to a fine powder. Sprinkle this and the red chilli powder over the yoghurt with some fresh chopped coriander. Refrigerate before serving.

6 Serve with tamarind chutney, which consists of ¾ of the tamarind water mixed with ¼ date water. These waters are made by soaking and squeezing the tamarind and dates and then sieving to discard the residue. Finally, season with salt and chilli.

Panipuri

INDIA'S FAVOURITE STREET FOOD, ALSO KNOWN AS GOLGAPPAS. MY MOST PRECIOUS MEMORY OF MY CHILDHOOD IS EATING GOLGAPPAS AT THE SUPREME HOTEL IN NAIROBI EVERY SATURDAY EVENING AS A TREAT

Preparation time: 20 minutes
Cooking time: 60 minutes
Serves 8

For the puris:

◇ ¼ cup plain wheat flour
◇ 2 tbsp urad dahl flour
◇ 1½ cups fine semolina
◇ Salt to taste
◇ Water to bind
◇ Cooking oil to fry

For the sauce (pani):

◇ 250-500g tamarind
◇ Water for boiling
◇ Black salt to taste
◇ 2 tbsp fresh ground cumin seeds
◇ 1 tbsp red chilli powder
◇ Sugar or jaggery to taste

To serve:

◇ 1-2 boiled potatoes, diced and mixed with fresh coriander
◇ 1 diced onion mixed with fresh coriander
◇ 1 cup boiled chick peas mixed with fresh coriander

Method for puri

1 Mix the flours and semolina. Add salt. Using a small amount of water at a time, make the dough. The dough should be stiff.

2 Place a damp cloth over the dough and leave for 20-30 minutes. Knead well to smoothen it.

3 Roll out into a big circle to thickness of a puri, approximately 6mm. Then, using a cutter about 1in or 2.5cm in diameter, cut out small discs.

4 Deep fry a few of the discs at a time in hot oil. To check if the oil is hot enough, drop a small amount of dough into the oil and if it sizzles and floats to the surface immediately, then the oil is at the correct temperature for frying. Take the small dough discs and gently slide them from the side of the pan into the hot oil. After a few seconds, press them carefully using a slotted ladle and flick hot oil onto them. This enhances it to puff up completely. Turn over the puris to cook the other side. They should be a golden colour with a crisp top. Repeat for the rest of the dough.

5 Store in an airtight container when cold.

Chef's tip

To enjoy the explosion of flavours, put the entire stuffed panipuri into your mouth.

Method for the pani

1 Boil the tamarind in some water and let it soak. (This can be done the day before or you can buy ready-made tamarind sauce.) After soaking the fresh tamarind, it is squeezed to extract all the sauce by straining through a sieve. This is the concentrated sauce. Add about 250-300ml water to this and bring to boil.

2 Add all the spices, sugar or jaggery and taste. Refrigerate this sauce and serve cold.

3 If the puris are not crisp, warm them in an oven for 10 minutes before serving.

4 To assemble the panipuri, lightly press the top of the puri to make a hole. Stuff with small amounts of diced and boiled potatoes, diced onions, boiled chickpeas and top with the tamarind sauce.

Bread-crumbed prawns

TOTALLY IRRESISTIBLE WHEN SPLASHED WITH GREEN CHUTNEY

Preparation time: 10 minutes
Cooking time: 15 minutes
Serves 4

You will need:

◇ *300g prawns*
◇ *1 cup cake flour*
◇ *1 egg beaten*
◇ *1-2 cups breadcrumbs*
◇ *Salt to taste*
◇ *Cooking oil to fry*

Method

1 Shell and de-vein the prawns. Remove the heads but keep the tails.

2 Slice the prawns open into butterfly shapes.

3 Dip each prawn in the flour, then into the beaten egg and roll them in the breadcrumbs.

4 Deep fry in medium-heated oil. Excessively heated oil may burn the breadcrumbs.

5 Remove the cooked prawns and then refry them in hot oil to make them crispy.

6 Serve with soy and chilli sauce or some green chutney.

Vada

CRISPY, SAVOURY BALLS THAT ARE A TYPICAL SOUTH INDIAN SNACK

Preparation time: 15 minutes
Cooking time: 20-25 minutes
Serves 6-8

You will need:

◇ 1 cup maize flour
◇ ¼ cup cake flour
◇ 1 tbsp semolina
◇ 1 tbsp oil
◇ 1 tsp fresh crushed green chillies
◇ 1 tsp fresh crushed ginger
◇ ¼ tsp turmeric
◇ ¼ tsp citric acid (optional)
◇ 1 tsp salt
◇ ¾ cup boiling water
◇ ¼ cup plain yoghurt
◇ Cooking oil to fry

Method

1 Mix the maize and cake flours, add the semolina and oil and combine to make a crumb consistency.

2 Add the chillies, ginger, turmeric powder and citric acid.

3 Add salt to the boiling water, then pour the water into the flour mixture and mix well. Lastly, add the yoghurt and mix again.

4 Cover and leave overnight. The following day, taste and adjust accordingly.

5 Heat the oil in a pan or karahi.

6 Take 1 tbsp of the batter at a time and slide it into the heated oil. It should float quickly to the top if the temperature is right.

7 Fry until medium brown in colour. Drain onto a paper towel. Repeat with the remaining batter. Serve hot with chutney.

Leftover vadas can be used to make dahi vada by soaking them in hot water for an hour. Perpare the yoghurt by adding salt, red chillies and roasted cumin seed powder. Squeeze the water from the soaked vada and add to the prepared yoghurt. Sprinkle freshly chopped coriander and refrigerate before serving.

Crunchy cabbage salad

THIS IS AN INCREDIBLY FLAVOUR-PACKED SALAD THAT'S BEST SAVOURED ON A HOT SUMMER'S DAY

Preparation time: 20 minutes
Serves 4-6

You will need:

◇ *2 packets of 2-minute noodles, any flavour*
◇ *1 tbsp oil*
◇ *½ cup sesame seeds*
◇ *½ cup either peanuts, pecans or a mix*

◇ *½ a medium cabbage shredded*
◇ *1 bunch of spring onions finely chopped*

For the dressing:

◇ *½ cup vinegar*
◇ *½ cup brown sugar*
◇ *½ cup extra virgin olive oil*

Method

1 First, make the dressing. Mix all the ingredients together in an airtight container until the sugar dissolves. This dressing will stay in the fridge for several weeks.

2 Crush the noodles and mix in the flavouring which comes with the noodles.

3 Dry fry the noodles gently in oil over a low heat until they are golden brown.

4 Roast the sesame seeds and nuts in a frying pan on a medium heat.

5 Mix the roasted seeds and nuts with the noodles. (This mixture can be stored in an airtight container for several weeks.)

6 Mix together the cabbage and the onions. Pour the dressing and the noodles/nut combination just before serving to retain the crunchiness of the salad. You will have enough dressing for more than one portion of the salad, so store the leftovers in the fridge and use when required.

Chicken tandoori style

TANDOORI CHICKEN IS AN ICONIC DISH, ALMOST EVERYONE KNOWS OF IT

Preparation: 15 minutes
Marinating time: 3-4 hours or overnight
Cooking time: 20 minutes
Serves 4

You will need:

◇ 2 tbsp fresh crushed garlic
◇ 1 tbsp fresh crushed ginger
◇ 1 tsp red chilli powder
◇ Salt to taste
◇ ½ cup yoghurt
◇ 2 tbsp lemon juice
◇ 1kg chicken washed and cut in pieces
◇ A pinch of tandoori colour
◇ 1 tsp cumin seeds
◇ 2 tbsp cooking oil
◇ Freshly chopped coriander to garnish
◇ 1 small onion cut in rings to garnish

Method

1 Mix together the garlic, ginger, chilli powder, salt, yoghurt, lemon juice, tandoori colour with 1 tbsp oil and marinate the chicken (slit the chicken to absorb the marinade) in this for a 3-4 hours or overnight.

2 Heat 1 tbsp oil, add the cumin seeds. As the seeds start to pop add the marinated chicken. Cover the pot until the chicken releases water.

3 Remove the lid from the pot and allow the chicken to cook and the water to evaporate.

4 Garnish with coriander and raw onion rings and serve hot.

Alternatively, instead of cooking this dish in a pot, leave out the cumin seeds and barbecue the marinated chicken on a hot grill. You can use chicken leg and wing portions, using this method, to create delicious finger foods or starters.

Khandvi

A FINGER FOOD DELICACY WHICH PROVIDES A REAL COOKING CHALLENGE

Preparation time: 10 minutes
Cooking time: 40 minutes
Serves 5

You will need:

◇ *1 cup gram flour*
◇ *1 tbsp cake flour*
◇ *1 cup plain yoghurt*
◇ *1¾ cups water*
◇ *1 tsp fresh crushed green chillies*
◇ *½ tsp fresh crushed ginger*
◇ *¼ tsp fresh crushed garlic*
◇ *A pinch of turmeric powder*
◇ *1 tsp each of salt, sugar, citric acid powder*

For the tadka:

◇ *I tsp each mustard and sesame seeds*
◇ *3 tbsp cooking oil*
◇ *Desiccated coconut and freshly chopped coriander to decorate*

Method

1 In a blender, mix together the gram flour, cake flour, yoghurt, water, chillies, ginger, garlic, turmeric powder, salt, sugar and citic acid powder. Taste. If it's not sour enough, add more citric acid. Put half of this mixture in a stainless steel pot and cover. Place on a steam stand in a pressure cooker with water.

2 Now pressure cook for 20 minutes. Cool and remove from the cooker and stir well. (Alternatively, the blended mixture can be cooked in a heavy-bottom frying pan, stirring all the time to ensure sure no lumps form. Keep stirring until mixture starts leaving the side of the pan.)

3 Using an old credit card or non-stick spatula, spread the mixture over the kitchen worktop evenly and thinly, so that it's around 1mm in thickness. (Alternatively, cover the mixture with plastic paper and roll out evenly.) Allow to dry for 4-5 minutes. Steam the second half of the mixture in the same way.

4 Cut long, even strips on the spread-out mixture for the width of the roll. Using your fingers, roll each strip so that it resembles tiny swiss rolls. Place in a serving dish. Repeat with remaining mixture. These can be left in the fridge overnight.

5 Before serving, remove from the fridge and leave at room temperature for 30 minutes. For the tadka, heat ½ cup oil, add mustard seeds. When the seeds start to pop, add the sesame seeds and pour over the khandvi. Sprinkle desiccated coconut and fresh coriander on top to decorate.

Spare ribs Chinese style

THE SOY SAUCE AND HONEY GIVE THIS DISH A CHINESE INFLUENCE

Preparation time: 10 minutes
Marination time: 4 hours or preferably overnight
Cooking time: 30-50 minutes
Serves 4

You will need:

◇ *1 rack of ribs (1.5kg)*
◇ *6 tbsp soy sauce*
◇ *3 tbsp honey*
◇ *2 tbsp brandy*
◇ *1 tsp salt*
◇ *A pinch of white pepper*

Method

1 Remove the flap and extra fat from the ribs and score all over with a sharp knife.

2 Line a baking tray with foil and lay the racks of ribs inside.

3 Mix the rest of the ingredients together. Then, using your hands rub this marinade mix into the ribs. Leave to marinate for at least 4 hours, but overnight is best.

4 Preheat the oven and bake the ribs for 30-50 minutes at 160°C/325°F/Gas Mark 4.

5 Add water if the sauce starts to evaporate.

6 During baking time, baste the ribs and turn them over several times. Serve hot.

Dhokla

DHOKLA HAILS FROM THE GUJARAT STATE. TRADITIONALLY IT IS PREPARED FROM CHICKPEAS OR GRAM FLOUR, BUT THIS RECEIPE USES SEMOLINA

Preparation time: 10 minutes
Cooking time: 25 minutes
Serves 4-6

You will need:

◇ ½ cup semolina
◇ 2 tbsp gram flour
◇ ½ cup plain yoghurt
◇ 1 tsp salt
◇ ½ tsp fresh crushed green chillies
◇ ½ tsp fresh crushed garlic
◇ ½ tsp fresh crushed ginger
◇ ½ tsp sugar
◇ A pinch of bicarbonate of soda
◇ 1 heaped tsp Eno fruit salts
◇ A sprinkle of red chilli powder

For the tadka:

◇ 1 tbsp cooking oil
◇ 1 tsp mustard seeds
◇ 1 tsp sesame seeds
◇ Freshly chopped coriander to garnish

Method

1 Fill the base of a steamer or rice cooker with water and cover. Bring to the boil and allow to simmer.

2 To make the batter, mix together all the ingredients except for the Eno (fruit salts) and the tadka.

3 Grease a deep 8in plate (or a size that would fit in the steamer). Add the Eno fruit salts to the batter mixture and mix well. Pour onto the greased plate.

4 Sprinkle over some red chilli powder and place in the steamer. Allow to steam for at least 15-20 minutes. Remove the plate and set aside.

5 For the tadka, heat the oil and add mustard seeds. When these begin to pop, add the sesame seeds. Pour this oil over the steamed dhokla. Garnish with the chopped coriander. Cut into squares and serve with coriander chutney.

Corn dhokla

PERFECT FOR BREAKFAST OR A SNACK

Preparation time:
Soak overnight
Cooking time:
25 minutes
Serves 6

You will need:

◇ 2 cups semolina
◇ 1 cup gram flour
◇ 1 tsp each of fresh crushed ginger and garlic
◇ 1 tsp fresh crushed green chillies
◇ ¼ tsp turmeric powder
◇ 1 tsp salt
◇ ¼ tsp citric acid
◇ 1 tbsp cooking oil

◇ 1½ cups ½ yoghurt and ½ cup warm water mix (diluted yoghurt)
◇ 400g can sweetcorn, drained
◇ 2 heaped tsp Eno fruit salts
◇ A sprinkle of red chilli powder

For the tadka:

◇ 3 tbsp cooking oil
◇ 1 tsp mustard seeds
◇ 1 tsp sesame seeds
◇ Freshly chopped coriander to garnish

Method

1 Mix the semolina, gram flour, ginger, garlic, chillies, turmeric, salt, citric acid and oil, until crumbly. Add the yoghurt until the consistency is firm but falls out of your hand quite easily. Add the corn and leave overnight.

2 The following day, taste and adjust salt. Add water if the consistency is hard. Fill the base of a steamer with water and cover. Bring to the boil and simmer.

3 Grease a deep 8in plate (or a size that would fit in the steamer). Add 1 tsp Eno fruit salts to ½ the batter mixture and mix well. Pour onto the greased plate.

4 Sprinkle over red chilli powder and place in the steamer. Allow to steam cook for at least 15-20 minutes. Repeat with the other ½ of the batter.

5 For the tadka, heat the oil, add mustard seeds. When these begin to pop add the sesame seeds. Pour this oil over the dhokla. Garnish with coriander.

6 Cut into squares and serve with coriander chutney.

Handwa (Handvo)

A STEAMED CAKE MADE OF RICE FLOUR AND LENTILS

Preparation time:
30 minutes or
soak overnight
Cooking time:
30 minutes
Serves 6

You will need:

◇ 1 cup toor dahl
◇ ¼ cup channa dahl
◇ ¼ cup urad dahl
◇ 2 cups rice flour
◇ ½ cup wheat flour

◇ 1 tsp salt
◇ 1 tsp fresh crushed green chillies
◇ 1 tsp fresh crushed ginger
◇ 1 tsp fresh crushed garlic
◇ 1 tsp sugar
◇ 1 cup plain yoghurt
◇ 1 cup diced cabbage
◇ 2 tbsp cooking oil
◇ 2 tsp sesame seeds

Method

1 Handwa flour can be bought ready-made or prepared at home by soaking the 3 dahls for 2-3 hours and then grinding them all together. Add the rice flour and the wheat flour and mix. Leave this overnight.

2 The following day, add the salt, chillies, ginger, garlic, sugar, yoghurt and cabbage and mix. Leave for 2-3 hours. If using ready-made handwa flour, mix all the spices, sugar, yoghurt and cabbage to 1 cup handwa flour. Leave for 1-2 hours. You might need to add water to achieve the right consistency, which is that of a cake mix.

3 Heat 2 tbsp cooking oil in an oven-proof dish and add 1 tsp sesame seeds. When the seeds start to pop add the mixture to it and mix well.

4 Sprinkle the remaining sesame seeds over the top and bake in a preheated oven at 180°C/350°F/Gas Mark 4 for 30-45minutes.

5 When cooled, cut into squares and serve.

Chicken salad Thai style

A TANTALISING AND HEALTHY SALAD WITH A HOT KICK

Preparation time: 15 minutes
Cooking time: 20 minutes
Serves 4

You will need:

◇ 2 chicken breasts cut into small cubes
◇ 1 tbsp soy sauce
◇ ½ tsp freshly crushed ginger
◇ A pinch of sugar
◇ ½ packet rice noodles boiled and strained

For the salad:

◇ 1 grated carrot
◇ 1 red pepper chopped small
◇ ½ cucumber chopped small
◇ ½ bunch of spring onions
◇ 1 cup bean sprouts

For the sauce:

◇ ½ tsp each fresh crushed garlic and ginger
◇ 3 tbsp lemon juice
◇ 4 tsp sugar
◇ 2 tsp soy sauce
◇ 1 tsp hot sauce (Tabasco)
◇ 1-2 tsp sesame oil
◇ Freshly chopped coriander to garnish

Method

1 Marinate the chicken in soy sauce, crushed ginger and sugar for about 10 minutes.

2 Stir fry in a wok or a pan until cooked. Keep aside.

3 Prepare the salad by mixing together all the salad ingredients.

4 Add the cooked chicken to the salad. Mix in the noodles.

5 Prepare the sauce by mixing together all the sauce ingredients and pour this onto the mixed salad just before serving.

6 Garnish with fresh coriander and serve.

Corn chevdo

CORN IS A HEALTHY GRAIN THAT IS ALSO RICH IN VITAMIN C AND IS ONE OF THE BEST SOURCES OF DIETARY FIBRE, TOO

Preparation time: 15 minutes
Cooking time: 15 minutes
Serves 4

You will need:

◇ *4-5 tbsp of oil (2-3 tbsp for the can)*
◇ *½ tsp mustard seeds*
◇ *6 fresh white corn grated*
◇ *or 400g can creamed sweetcorn*
◇ *Salt to taste*
◇ *A pinch of turmeric*
◇ *1 tsp fresh crushed green chillies*
◇ *1 tsp fresh crushed garlic*
◇ *½ cup milk*
◇ *Freshly chopped coriander to garnish*
◇ *Sev to serve*
◇ *1 lemon sliced into 4 to serve*

Method

1 Heat the oil and add mustard seeds. When the seeds start to pop add the grated corn or the canned sweetcorn.

2 Add the salt, turmeric, chillies, garlic and mix well.

3 Cook on a medium heat for 10-15 minutes, stirring frequently.

4 Add the milk, then turn down the heat and simmer for 2-3 minutes.

5 Garnish with chopped coriander and serve hot with sev and lemon.

Dhebra

AN IDEAL SNACK OR BREAKFAST DISH

Preparation time:
Soak overnight
Cooking time: 40 minutes
Serves 6-8

You will need:

◇ 1½ cups maize
or corn flour
◇ 1 cup cake flour
◇ ½ cup yoghurt
◇ 1 tsp carom seeds
◇ 1 tsp sesame seeds
◇ 1 tsp salt
◇ 1 tsp oil
◇ ½ cup corn starch
(optional)
◇ ½ cup tamarind
sauce (optional)
◇ 1 tsp fresh crushed
garlic
◇ 1 tsp fresh crushed
green chillies
◇ 1 tsp fresh crushed
ginger
◇ 1 cup fresh fenugreek
leaves (methi) cleaned
and chopped
◇ Warm water
◇ Cooking oil to fry

Method

1 Sieve the maize flour and add the cake flour.

2 Add yoghurt, carom and sesame seeds, salt, oil and the tamarind sauce.

3 Mix in the spices and fenugreek leaves. Add a small amount of warm water at a time to bind it to a soft dough. Leave overnight.

4 Using greaseproof paper, pinch about 1 tsp of dough and pat it with your fingers into a small circle. To make them less oily dip the small circle into corn starch before frying (optional).

5 To check if the oil is hot enough, drop a small amount of dough into the oil and if it sizzles and floats to the surface immediately, then the oil is at the correct temperature for frying. Take the patted dough and gently slide it from the side of the pan into the hot oil. After a few seconds press it gently using a slotted ladle and flick hot oil onto it. This puffs it up. Turn it over to the other side until golden brown. Remove and drain on a paper towel. Repeat with remaining dough. Serve hot.

Kebabs

A GREAT FAVORITE, THESE TASTE JUST DIVINE WHEN BARBECUED

Preparation time:
10 minutes
Cooking time:
20 minutes
Serves 6-8

You will need:

◇ 1 tbsp fresh
crushed garlic
◇ 1 tbsp fresh
crushed ginger
◇ 1 tbsp fresh
crushed green chillies
◇ 1-2 slices of bread
soaked in water, until
soft, then mashed
(this helps to bind
the meat)
◇ 1 tbsp salt
◇ 500g minced lamb
or minced beef
◇ 1 onion diced
◇ 1 bunch spring
onions diced
◇ Freshly chopped
coriander
◇ 1 tbsp oil

Method

1 Add the garlic, ginger, chillies, mashed bread mixture and salt to the minced meat. Mix well.

2 Take a pinch of the mixture and microwave for a few seconds. Taste for salt and adjust.

3 When ready to cook, add the onions, spring onions and the coriander and mix well. Make small balls out of this mixture.

4 In a shallow pot or frying pan, heat the oil and add these balls. Cover the pan and cook over a medium heat. Shake the pan to stir the balls. When the water dries out, the kebabs should be ready to serve.

5 Serve with tamarind chutney a green salad and some naan.

For sheekh kebabs, use the above recipe for the mixture, but instead of cooking it in a pan, cook over a charcoal fire on a skewer. The same mixture can be used to make spicy burgers.

Bhelpuri and Mexican bhel

BHELPURI IS THE MOST COMMONLY SOLD CHAAT IN THE STREETS OF MUMBAI, WHERE IT IS CALLED THE INDIAN SALAD

Preparation time: 20 minutes
Cooking time: 10 minutes
Serves 6

You will need:

- ◇ *1 cup puffed rice*
- ◇ *1 cup thin sev*
- ◇ *1 cup of crisp puri (broken up)*
- ◇ *2 tbsp chopped coriander*
- ◇ *2 boiled potatoes diced*
- ◇ *1 onion diced*
- ◇ *1 cup boiled chickpeas*
- ◇ *1 chopped raw mango (optional)*
- ◇ *1 cup boiled moong lentils*
- ◇ *Coriander chutney*
- ◇ *Tamarind sauce (see Panipuri, page 18)*

Method

1 Mix the puffed rice, sev and puri in a large bowl.

2 Divide the chopped coriander into 5 equal amounts and mix each portion with the potatoes, onions, chickpeas, mango and moong, separately.

3 Serve these in individual bowls.

4 To assemble the bhel, take 1-2 tbsp of the puffed rice, sev and puri mixture with 1 tsp each of the potatoes, onions, chickpeas, mango and moong. Mix with 1 tsp chutney and tamarind sauce.

For Mexican bhel, substitute puffed rice, sev and puris with broken up tortillas and in addition serve a bowl of guacamole, chopped red chillies and some fresh lemon slices.

Chef's tip

If you find your puffed rice has lost some of its crispness, try roasting it to get the freshness back.

Patra leaves

COLOCASIA LEAVES, ALSO KNOWN AS ELEPHANT EARS, GROW IN
ABUNDANCE IN MY GARDEN. THEY'RE A GREAT SOURCE OF IRON

Preparation time: 40 minutes
Cooking time: 15-20 minutes
Serves 6-8

For the paste:

◇ 1 tbsp oil
◇ 3 cups gram flour
◇ 1 tbsp fresh crushed green chillies
◇ ½ cup tamarind pulp
◇ 3 tbsp sugar or grated jaggery
◇ ½ tsp carom seeds
◇ Salt to taste
◇ 1 tbsp crushed fresh garlic
◇ 1 tsp red chilli powder

For the rolls:

◇ 10-15 small to medium patra leaves, washed and dried
◇ 2 tbsp desiccated coconut to garnish
◇ Freshly chopped coriander to garnish

For the tadka:

◇ 1 tbsp oil
◇ 1 tsp mustard seeds
◇ 1 sliced onion
◇ 1 tsp sesame seeds

Method for the paste

1 Mix all the ingredients together and add water a little at a time to make a thick paste.

2 Taste and adjust for salt. Leave aside.

Method for the rolls

1 Place each leaf vein side up and using a sharp knife, slice off the thick central vein. Wash and dry the leaves.

2 Now, make a slit at the end of each leaf so that it lies flat.

3 Place the first leaf on a flat surface. Carefully using your fingers, spread a thin layer of paste over it. Now place the second leaf on the first one, but with the tip of the second leaf on the opposite side of the first leaf. Spread the paste in the same manner on this second leaf and repeat this process for another 2-3 leaves. Four leaves at a time make a reasonably sized

roll but it depends on the original size of the leaf, so use your discretion.

4 Roll up the layered leaves together tightly starting from the pointed tip.

5 Continue making the rolls with the rest of the leaves, and then using a steamer or pressure cooker, steam these rolls for 10-15 minutes. When the cooked rolls are cool cut in 2cm thick slices and keep aside.

6 Once cooled, the steamed patra rolls can be frozen for use at a later stage. The steamed rolls can also be eaten with a drizzle of oil.

Method for the tadka

1 Heat the oil and add mustard seeds. When these begin to pop, add the onion.

2 Once the onion turns slightly brown, add the sliced patra and sesame seeds and mix well. Cook for 5 minutes.

3 Serve hot, garnished with chopped coriander and desiccated coconut.

The sliced steamed patra can also be deep fried and served with green chutney.

Sev press

MAKE YOUR OWN SNACKS SUCH AS SEV AND OTHER INDIAN DELICACIES WITH A HEAVY-DUTY BRASS SEV MAKER

The sev press is a special piece of equipment for making sev, thika gathia, soft gathia and chakri. Typically made from brass (as shown above), you can also get stainless steel varieties. It comes with discs with different sized holes and slits. The most common are ones with a small hole (for making sev), one with a larger hole (for making thika gathia), one with a star shape (for making chakri and soft gathia) and one with slits (for making papri gathia). The sev press often gets passed down to each generation and lasts a lifetime.

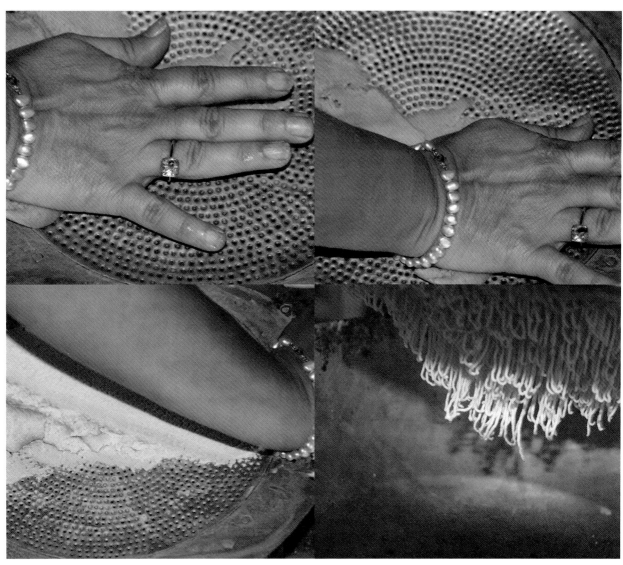

Jaro

Alternatively you can use a jaro instead of a sev press. This is a big metal sieve with holes (as shown above and right). It also comes with star-shaped holes, larger holes and slits. It is mainly used when making large quantities of sev.

Sev

A VERMICELLI-LIKE SNACK USED AS A TOPPING IN MOST CHAAT RECIPES

Preparation time: 20 minutes
Cooking time: 25 minutes

You will need:

◇ *1 cup water*
◇ *2 tsp salt*
◇ *2 tsp white chilli powder*
◇ *¼ tsp asafetida*
◇ *500g gram flour*
◇ *2 tsp oil*
◇ *Cooking oil to fry*

Method

1 Boil some water and dissolve the salt in it. Add chilli powder and asafetida to the gram flour and mix. Add oil and mix again.

2 Now add a little water at a time, mixing thoroughly, and knead to a smooth dough. The dough should be somewhere in between soft and stiff. Grease the dough using ½ tbsp oil.

3 Take the sev press (see page 38) and the disc with the small holes and place it at the bottom of the press. Lightly rub oil on the inside of the press. Place the dough inside it. Close the machine tightly.

4 Heat oil in a frying pan or karahi over a medium flame. To check if the oil is hot enough, drop a small amount of dough into the oil and if it sizzles and floats to the surface immediately, then the oil is at the correct temperature for frying. Hold the machine over oil and turn the handle of the machine to force the dough through the disc. Move machine in circular motion over the oil and turn the handle continuously.

5 Fry until the sev is pale yellow in colour. Remove and place in a colander lined with paper towel to drain off any excess oil. Repeat the process for the rest of the dough.

6 Store in an airtight container to keep the sev crispy.

You can use a jaro instead of a sev press (see page 39). Place over a pan of hot oil. Carefully take some dough and rub it across the jaro so that the dough falls through the holes into the oil. Remove the sieve and fry the sev till they turn a pale yellow in colour.

Papri gathia

CRISP AND TANGY BITE-SIZE SNACKS THAT GO WELL WITH DRINKS

Preparation: 20 minutes
Cooking time: 1 hour

You will need:

◇ 6-7 medium potatoes
◇ 2-3 tsp salt
◇ 2 tsp white chilli powder
◇ 2 tbsp ground carom seeds
◇ A pinch of asafetida
◇ 1kg gram flour
◇ Cooking oil to fry

Method

1 Boil the potatoes, peel and mash finely. Add salt, chilli powder, carom seeds, and asafetida to the gram flour.

2 Add the mashed potatoes and mix thoroughly. Mix in the oil. The dough must be without any lumps. A mincing machine or blender can be used to achieve this.

3 Take the sev press and the disc with slits and place it at the bottom of the sev press. Lightly rub oil on the inside of the press. Place the dough in it. Close the machine tightly.

4 Heat some oil in a pan over a medium flame. To check if the oil is hot enough, drop a small amount of dough into the oil and if it sizzles and floats to the surface immediately, then the oil is at the correct temperature for frying. Holding the press over the oil, turn the handle to force the dough through the disc. Move the press in a circular motion over the oil and turn the handle continuously.

5 Fry until the papri is light yellow in colour. Remove and place in a colander lined with paper towels to drain off any excess oil. Repeat the process for the rest of the dough. Store in an airtight container.

You can use a jaro instead of a sev press (see page 39).

Tikha gathia

TASTES GREAT WITH APERITIF DRINKS

Preparation time: 20 minutes
Cooking time: 25 minutes

You will need:

◇ 750g gram flour
◇ 1 tsp carom seeds
◇ 2 tsp red chilli powder
◇ 2½ tsp salt
◇ ¼ cup oil
◇ ½ cup water
◇ Cooking oil to fry

Method

1 Mix gram flour, carom seeds, chilli powder and salt. Knead to a smooth dough by adding water.

2 Using the sev press place the disc with large holes at the bottom of the press. Lightly rub oil on the inside of the press. Place the dough in it. Close the machine tightly.

3 Heat some oil in a pan over a medium flame. To check if the oil is hot enough, drop a small amount of dough into the oil and if it sizzles and floats to the surface immediately, then the oil is at the correct temperature for frying. Hold the machine over the oil and turn the handle to force the dough through the disc. Move the press in a circular motion and turn the handle continuously.

4 Fry until the gathia is reddish in colour.

5 Remove and place in a colander lined with a paper towel to drain excess oil. Repeat the process. Store in an airtight container.

You can use a jaro instead of a sev press (see page 39). Place over a pan of hot oil. Carefully take some dough and rub it across the jaro so that the dough falls through the holes into the oil. Fry the gathia till they turn a reddish colour.

Mathi

AN ANYWHERE, ANYTIME SNACK

Preparation time: 10 minutes
Cooking time: 20 minutes

You will need:

◊ *100g ghee*
◊ *Salt to taste*
◊ *1 tbsp coarse ground pepper (optional)*
◊ *1 tbsp carom seeds*
◊ *400g cake flour*
◊ *Lukewarm water*
◊ *Cooking oil to fry*

Method

1 Mix the ghee, salt, pepper and carom seeds with the flour. Add lukewarm water a little at a time and knead to a soft and smooth dough.

2 Divide this into 4-5 pieces and roll each piece into a large circle, about 3-4mm thick. Spread a pinch of ghee onto this and roll like a swiss roll.

3 Cut the roll into 2cm pieces. Repeat with the rest of the dough. Then, roll each 2cm piece into a circle, about 5cm in diameter.

4 Prick the surface a few times with a fork to prevent it from puffing up during the cooking process. Keep aside and roll a few more.

5 Meanwhile, heat the oil in a karahi to a medium heat. To test the temperature is right, drop a tiny ball of dough into the oil and if it sizzles and rises quickly to the top, this indicates that the oil is ready. Do not heat the oil too much as the mathi will turn brown quickly and remain uncooked.

6 Add 6-8 of the pricked mathi into the oil. Gently fry, turning and flipping often until the mathis are light brown in colour. Remove from the oil onto paper towels to drain.

7 Allow to cool at room temperature. Store in airtight containers.

Granola

HOMEMADE GRANOLA IS A HEALTHY BREAKFAST AND SNACK FOOD

Preparation time:
20 minutes
Cooking time:
18-20 minutes

You will need:

◊ *6 cups crispy crunchy oats*
◊ *1½ cups chopped pecan nuts*
◊ *1½ cups chopped almonds*
◊ *1 cup desiccated coconut*
◊ *1 cup apple juice*
◊ *3 tbsp cooking oil*
◊ *3 tsp cinnamon powder*
◊ *1 tsp all spice mix*
◊ *½-¾ cup brown sugar*
◊ *3 cups mixed dried fruit, including cranberries*

Method

1 Mix the oats, nuts and coconut in a large bowl and keep aside.

2 In a pan, boil together the apple juice, cooking oil, cinnamon powder, all spice mix and the sugar.

3 Add the boiled mixture to the oat and nuts mixture and mix together well.

4 Bake this at 160°C/325°F/Gas Mark 4 for 15-20 minutes.

5 Remove from the oven. Add the dried fruit to the mixture and bake for a further 5 minutes.

6 Remove from the oven and allow to cool.

7 Store in an airtight container and serve for breakfast or as a snack.

Chakri

THESE GOLDEN, SPIRAL-SHAPED CRISPY BITES ARE PACKED FULL OF FLAVOUR

Preparation time: 20 minutes
Cooking time: 60 minutes

You will need:

◇ *2 medium potatoes*
◇ *3 tbsp butter*

◇ *500g rice flour*
◇ *Salt to taste*
◇ *1 tsp whole cumin seeds*
◇ *1 tsp sesame seeds*
◇ *1 tsp fresh crushed green chillies*
◇ *¾ cup plain yoghurt*
◇ *¼ cup water*
◇ *Cooking oil to fry*

Method

1 Boil and mash the potatoes. Add the rest of the ingredients and knead to a soft dough.

2 Take the sev press (see page 38) and the star disc and place it at the bottom of the sev press. Lightly rub oil on the inside of the press. Now add the dough inside it. Close the machine tightly. Move the machine in a circular motion and turn the handle continuously until you make a spiral circle. The dough will come out star-shaped. Gently press the ends of the spirals to stop the spiral from breaking.

3 Heat some oil in a frying pan or karahi over a medium flame. To check if the oil is hot enough, drop a small amount of dough into the oil and if it sizzles and floats to the surface immediately, then the oil is at the correct temperature for frying. Using a spatula, carefully pick up the spiralled dough and gently place into the pan. Fry until gold brown. Fry 3-4 of these sprials at a time turning over slowly to cook on both sides until golden brown and crispy. Try not to turn them too quickly as this might unwind the spiral.

4 Fry until the chakri is pale yellow in colour. Remove and place in a colander lined with paper towels to drain off any excess oil. Repeat the process for the rest of the dough.

5 Store in an airtight container to retain the freshness.

Food is a central activity of
mankind and one of the single
most significant trademarks
of a culture

MARK KURLANSKY

PICKLES &
CONDIMENTS
....

Cauliflower and carrot pickle

AN OIL-FREE, TANGY AND ZESTY CONDIMENT THAT'S LOW IN CALORIES

Preparation time: 15 minutes
Cooking time: 5 minutes

You will need:

◇ *1 small cauliflower*
◇ *500g carrots*
◇ *1 tbsp salt*
◇ *1 tbsp red chilli powder*
◇ *2 tbsp ground mustard seeds*
◇ *½ cup white vinegar*

Method

1 Cut the cauliflower into small florets and wash thoroughly.

2 Peel the carrots and slice them into long, thin pieces and wash.

3 Blanche them in hot water with the salt for about 2 minutes. Do not over boil as this will soften them too much.

4 Drain and cool.

5 Add the chilli powder, the ground mustard seeds and vinegar. Mix well.

6 Taste and adjust. Store in the fridge to use when required.

Coriander chutney

THERE IS NO DISH THAT CANNOT BE PEPPED UP WITH THIS CHUTNEY

Preparation time: 10 minutes

You will need:

- 1 bunch of coriander
- 1 tsp salt
- 1 tsp fresh ground green chillies
- 1 tsp fresh ground garlic
- 1 tsp cumin seeds
- ½ cup ground groundnuts
- 1 tbsp ground ghatia or sev (optional)
- 1 tsp sugar
- 2 tbsp lemon juice

Method

1 Wash and dry the coriander.

2 Mix with all the ingredients in a blender to a fine paste. If the chutney is too thick, dilute by adding water.

3 Taste and adjust for salt. The chutney should be hot and spicy.

Guacamole dip

THE CLASSIC MEXICAN DISH FUSED
WITH INDIAN SPICES

Preparation time: 15 minutes

You will need:

◇ *1 ripe avocado*
◇ *1 tsp fresh crushed green chillies*
◇ *1 tsp salt*
◇ *Juice of 1 lemon*
◇ *½ tsp fresh crushed garlic*
◇ *1 small onion diced in small cubes*
◇ *1 tomato diced in small cubes*
◇ *Freshly chopped coriander (optional)*

Method

1 Scoop out the ripe avocado.

2 Mash it with the back of a spoon or in a pestle and mortar.

3 Add the rest of the ingredients and mix well.

4 Taste and garnish with fresh chopped coriander and serve with nachos or hot pitta bread.

Tamarind chutney

THE SWEET, SOUR, TANGY TASTE
OF TAMARIND IS UNMISTAKABLE
AND EXTREMELY DELICIOUS
– REPUTED ALL OVER THE WORLD
FOR ITS MEDICINAL PROPERTIES

Preparation time: 10 minutes
Cooking time: 40 minutes

You will need:

◇ *200g tamarind (brown)*
◇ *200g pitted dates*
◇ *1 tbsp salt to taste (preferably black salt)*
◇ *1 tbsp red chilli powder*
◇ *1 tbsp roasted cumin powder*
◇ *Sugar or jaggery to taste*

Method

1 In a large pot boil the tamarind and dates in water. Reduce heat and cook for 30 minutes until the dates start to dissolve.

2 Remove from heat, allow the mixture to cool and sieve to remove the pulp. This mixture can be frozen and used when required for cooking or to prepare chutneys.

3 To make the chutney, place the sieved mixture back on the heat. Add salt, chilli powder, cumin powder and sugar or jaggery. Taste and adjust. The chutney should be sweet and sour and not too spicy.

4 Allow to cool before serving. It can also be frozen at this stage for later use.

Mango pickle

IN ZIMBABWE, THERE'S AN ABUNDANCE OF MANGOES IN DECEMEBER AND JANUARY – TIME FOR MAKING THIS DELICIOUS PICKLE

Preparation time: 45-50 minutes
Fermenting time: 3-7 days

You will need:

◇ 2½kg mangoes (round and firm)
◇ ¾ cup salt
◇ 1 tbsp turmeric powder
◇ 2 cups oil
◇ 2 tbsp red chillies (dry and whole)
◇ 2 tbsp cumin seeds
◇ 2 tbsp mustard seeds
◇ 2 tbsp asafetida
◇ ½ cup whole coriander ground
◇ ½ cup whole fennel
◇ ½ cup fenugreek seeds ground (methi)
◇ 2 tbsp whole cloves
◇ 2 tbsp cinnamon sticks
◇ 1 tbsp whole cardamom
◇ 1½kg jaggery

Method

1 Wash and cut the mangoes in small squares with the peel still on. Place in a large container with a lid and add ¾ cup salt and the turmeric powder and mix.

2 Stir occasionally until the mangoes are soft. This can take a couple of days. Place on a clean cloth in the sun or indoors for the mangoes to dry. The drying process can take up to 2 days. Warm the oil and add the whole red chillies and stir until the chillies darken in colour.

3 Add the cumin seeds, mustard seeds and asafetida. Add the rest of the ingredients and the jaggery to the soft dried mangoes and mix well. Then, pour the oil mixture to the mangoes and mix again.

4 Keep in the container for 2-3 days until the jaggery has melted and it is well mixed. Taste, and store in a glass jar ready to be served when required.

Alternatively, you can buy the mango pickle mix and combine 1-2 tbsp with 1 tbsp oil and sliced raw mangoes

Green chilli pickle

AN INDIAN CLASSIC THAT ENHANCES ANY DISH AND IS RICH IN VITAMIN C

Preparation time: 10 minutes
Cooking time: 5-10 minutes

You will need:

- ◇ 10-12 small green chillies
- ◇ 2 tbsp cooking oil
- ◇ 1 tsp asafetida
- ◇ 1 tsp mustard seeds
- ◇ 1 tbsp coarse salt

For the gram flour version:

- ◇ 10-12 small green chillies
- ◇ 1 tbsp oil
- ◇ 1 tsp mustard seeds
- ◇ 1 tbsp coarse salt
- ◇ 1 tbsp citric acid powder
- ◇ 1 tsp sugar
- ◇ 2-3 tsp gram flour

Method

1 Wash the whole chillies, slit lengthwise and remove the seeds.

2 Heat oil and add asafetida and mustard seeds. When the seeds start to pop add the salt and the seedless whole chillies. Cover and simmer for 2-3 minutes. Remove from heat.

3 Leave overnight. Store in a glass jar and use as a condiment.

Method for the gram flour

1 Wash the whole chillies, slit lengthwise and remove the seeds.

2 Heat the oil and add the mustard seeds. When the seeds start to pop add the salt, citric acid, sugar and whole chillies and stir. Add the gram flour and stir.

3 Remove from heat and cover the pan with a lid. After 1-2 minutes, give it a stir. The gram flour should have cooked. If it is still in powder form then put it back on the heat with a few drops of water, cover and simmer for 1-2 minutes before removing from heat. Cool and store in the fridge.

Cucumber yoghurt raita

A COOL AND REFRESHING CHUTNEY SOMETIMES USED TO TOP A FIERY CURRY

Preparation time: 15 minutes

You will need:

◇ ½ cucumber
◇ ¼ tsp salt
◇ ½ tsp fresh crushed green chillies
◇ 1 tsp ground mustard seeds
◇ 1 cup plain yoghurt
◇ Freshly chopped coriander to garnish

Method

1 Peel and grate the cucumber. Squeeze and drain off excess water.

2 Mix the salt, green chillies and ground mustard seeds into the yoghurt.

3 Add the squeezed cucumber and mix well.

4 Garnish with chopped coriander and serve.

Peanut and chilli chutney

A GREAT SPICY AND TASTY ACCOMPANIMENT TO ALL DISHES

Preparation time: 20 minutes
Cooking time: 5 minutes

You will need:

◇ 1 cup peanuts
◇ 2 tbsp cooking oil
◇ 1 tbsp cumin seeds
◇ 2 tsp crushed garlic
◇ 2 tbsp sesame seeds
◇ 6 fresh red chillies
◇ ½ cup desiccated coconut
◇ Juice of 4 lemons
◇ Salt to taste

Method

1 Shallow fry the peanuts in 1 tbsp oil.

2 Heat the remaining oil in a separate pot and add cumin seeds, crushed garlic, sesame seeds and the chillies.

3 Put the fried peanuts, the oil mixture and the desiccated coconut in an electric blender and whizz. Alternatively you can use a pestle and mortar and pound it to a coarse mixture.

4 Mix well with lemon juice and add salt.

5 Store in jar and keep in the fridge.

Lime pickle

ANOTHER DELICIOUSLY HEALTHY, OIL-FREE PICKLE THAT IS TO DIE FOR

Preparation time: 20 minutes
Cooking time: 15-20 minutes
Fermenting time: 5-7 days

You will need:

◇ *1kg fresh yellow lime*
◇ *2 tbsp salt*
◇ *A pinch of turmeric powder*
◇ *1-2 cups sugar*
◇ *½ cup red chilli powder*

Method

1 Wash and cut the lime into quarters. Boil these in hot water with salt and turmeric powder for about 15 minutes until the skin is tender.

2 Spread out on to a clean cloth and let them cool.

3 Place in a container and cover with a lid. Leave overnight to soften further.

4 The following day, boil the softened lime and the sugar for 10-15 minutes until the desired consistency of the syrup is achieved.

5 Remove from heat and add the chilli powder and mix well. Leave aside for 5-7 days to ferment stirring every day.

6 Taste for salt and add accordingly.

7 Store in the fridge in a glass jar and serve as a condiment.

Dried fruit pickle

THIS IS A SPICY, SWEET AND SOUR RELISH WITH AN EXQUISITE TASTE

Preparation time: 30 minutes
excluding soaking time
Cooking time: 30 minutes

You will need:

◇ *125g dried apricots*
◇ *125g each dried mango, apriocts, figs, peaches or prunes*
◇ *125g dried figs*
◇ *350g jaggery*
◇ *3 cups vinegar*
◇ *2 tbsp salt*
◇ *3 tbsp red chilli powder*

Method

1 Soak all the dried fruits, except the prunes, in half a cup of vinegar overnight.

2 The following day, drain off the vinegar and chop the fruit and the prunes into halves or quarters as desired, removing any seeds.

3 Mix the jaggery and the remaining vinegar, salt and chilli in a large pot and bring to boil. Continue boiling for another 5 minutes.

4 Add the fruit and boil for a further 5 minutes.

5 Lower heat and cook until the mixture thickens, stirring continuously to prevent from scorching.

6 Remove from heat and cool. Store in an airtight glass jar.

7 Serve with all Indian meals or cheese and crackers.

Garam masala

AN AROMATIC BLEND OF SPICES
WHICH IS FRAGRANT AND ENHANCES
FLAVOUR IN INDIAN COOKING

Preparation time: 15 minutes
Cooking time: 25 minutes

You will need:

◇ *100g cumin seeds*
◇ *200g coriander seeds*
◇ *1 whole nutmeg*
◇ *2 tbsp cardamom seeds*
◇ *1 tsp cloves*
◇ *½ cup cinnamon*
◇ *1 tbsp sesame seeds*
◇ *½ cup star anise*

Method

1 Roast all the spices together except star anise for about 10-15 minutes on medium heat, stirring from time to time until the ingredients have darkened slightly and give off a rich aroma. Remove from the pan and allow to cool.

2 Roast the star anise separately on medium heat in the same way for 5-10 minutes.

3 Mix together all the roasted ingredients and grind to a fine powder.

4 Store in an airtight container.

Red chilli powder

A GREAT FAVORITE FOR BARBECUES,
ITS TASTE AND FRESHNESS ARE AT
ITS BEST WHEN COOKED AND
SERVED IMMEDIATELY

Preparation time: 10 minutes
Cooking time: 10 minutes

You will need:

◇ *1kg whole red chillies*
◇ *1-2 tbsp cooking oil*

Method

1 Wash the red chillies, remove the seeds and wipe with a damp cloth.

2 Coat the chillies with a small amount of oil and place in a warm oven for about 5-10 minutes until crisp.

3 Grind this mixture to a granular form, not to a fine powder.

4 Mix in 1 tbsp oil and store in an airtight container.

I don't even know what my natural colour is, natural? What is natural? What is that? I do not believe in totally natural for women. For me, natural has something to do with vegetables

DONATELLA VERSACE

VEGETARIAN

Stuffed eggplant

COMMONLY KNOWN AS BRINJAL OR AUBERGINE, IT'S VERY NUTRITIOUS
AND ALSO SOMETIMES DESCRIBED AS THE POOR MAN'S MEAT

Preparation time: 10 minutes
Cooking time: 20 minutes
Serves 3-4

You will need:

◇ *300g baby eggplant*
◇ *1 whole chopped onion*
◇ *2 tbsp crushed peanuts*
◇ *1 tsp fresh crushed garlic*
◇ *1 tsp red chilli powder*
◇ *1 tsp cumin powder*
◇ *1 tsp garam masala*
◇ *1 tsp salt*
◇ *1 tbsp crushed sev or ghatia*
◇ *A pinch of sugar*
◇ *2 tbsp cooking oil*
◇ *½ tsp cumin seeds*
◇ *2 tomatoes chopped*
◇ *Freshly chopped coriander to garnish*

Method

1 Cut the stems off the eggplants and wash the eggplants. Cut two slits crosswise into each eggplant so it opens like a flower. Set aside.

2 In a bowl, mix the chopped onion, peanuts, crushed garlic, chilli powder, cumin powder, garam masala, salt, crushed sev or gathia and sugar with a little oil. Mix well. Stuff a small amount of this mixture at a time, into each of the eggplants.

3 Heat the remaining oil in a medium pan. Add cumin seeds. When they start to pop, add the eggplants. Cover and cook for 2-3 minutes.

4 Add the chopped tomatoes and mix gently. Cook on a low heat for 10 minutes. Check frequently and add a small amount of water if the mixture is too dry. To test if cooked, insert a knife into the eggplant and it should slide in and out easily.

5 Taste and garnish with chopped coriander before serving. Serve with roti.

Chef's tip

Raw eggplants have a bitter tatse. They become tender when cooked, developing a rich and complex flavour.

Bhinda

THE UNIQUE FLAVOR OF BHINDA CAN BE DESCRIBED AS ANYTHING FROM SILKY TO SLIMY! IT'S A TRADITIONAL VEGETARIAN DELICACY THAT NEEDS TO BE TASTED TO BE APPRECIATED FULLY

Preparation time: 10 minutes
Cooking time: 10 minutes
Serves 4

You will need:
- *200g bhinda*
- *1 sliced onion*
- *1 tsp salt*
- *1 tsp red chilli powder*
- *½ tsp fresh crushed garlic*
- *½ tsp turmeric powder*
- *2-3 tbsp cooking oil*
- *Freshly chopped coriander to garnish*

Method

1 Soak and wash the bhinda in water, pat them dry and cut them into long strips.

2 Place all the ingredients in a microwave-proof dish and mix well.

3 Cover the dish and microwave for 5 minutes. Remove and stir well. Repeat until the bhinda is cooked. You can microwave them for a little longer if you prefer them crispy.

4 Garnish with some coriander and serve hot with roti.

Potatoes with tomatoes

A SIMPLE AND EASY EVERYDAY DISH THAT IS POPULAR IN INDIAN KITCHENS

Preparation time: 10 minutes
Cooking time: 15 minutes
Serves 4

You will need:

◇ *3-4 medium potatoes*
◇ *1 tbsp cooking oil*
◇ *1 tsp mustard seeds*
◇ *1 tsp fresh crushed garlic*
◇ *2 large tomatoes liquidised*
or 400g can peeled tomatoes
◇ *Salt to taste*
◇ *1 tbsp sugar or grated jaggery*
◇ *1 tbsp red chilli powder*
◇ *2 tbsp tamarind pulp*
◇ *Freshly chopped coriander to garnish*

Method

1 Boil the potatoes until cooked. Peel and dice each potato into quarters and put aside to cool.

2 Heat the oil in a frying pan and add the mustard seeds. When the seeds start to pop, add the garlic and the liquidised tomatoes.

3 Add salt, sugar or grated jaggery, red chilli powder and tamarind pulp. Stir and allow to cook for about 10 minutes.

4 Taste and adjust accordingly.

5 Finally add the diced boiled potatoes and 2-3 tbsp water to this sauce. Mix gently to avoid the potatoes from breaking.

6 Garnish with coriander and serve hot with roti.

Spaghetti a la fabio

MY INDIAN-FUSED ITALIAN DISH IS NAMED AFTER A VERY GOOD ITALIAN FRIEND OF MINE

Preparation time: 25 minutes
Cooking time: 20 minutes
Serves 2-3

You will need:

◇ *2 tbsp olive oil*
◇ *1 tsp fresh crushed garlic*
◇ *3 large tomatoes liquidised*
or 400g can peeled tomatoes
◇ *Salt to taste*
◇ *1 tsp red chilli powder*
◇ *1 tsp paprika powder*
◇ *¼ cup fresh cream*
◇ *A tot of vodka (optional)*
◇ *250g spaghetti*
◇ *Grated cheese to serve*

Method

1 To make the sauce, heat 1 tbsp oil with the garlic.

2 As the garlic starts to sizzle, add the tomatoes. salt, chilli and paprika.

3 Simmer for a few minutes until the tomatoes are blended well.

4 Mix in the cream and vodka on a low heat.

5 In a separate pot, boil the spaghetti in hot water with 1 tsp salt and oil. Keep checking the pasta until it is al dente – this is when there is a little bite left in the centre.

6 Drain and serve with the cooked sauce and grated cheese.

Channa masala

A POPULAR PUNJABI DISH OFTEN EATEN WITH BHATURA. THE COMPLETE DISH IS KNOWN AS CHOLE BHATURE

Preparation time: 10 minutes
not including overnight soaking
Cooking time: 30 minutes
Serves 4

You will need:

◇ *1 cup dry channa (chickpeas)*
or 400g can cooked channa
◇ *1 large onion diced*
◇ *2 tbsp cooking oil*
◇ *1 large tomato grated or blended*
or 400g can peeled tomatoes
◇ *1 tsp fresh crushed garlic*
◇ *2 tsp fresh crushed ginger*
◇ *1 tsp fresh crushed green chillies*
◇ *1 tbsp tamarind sauce*
◇ *1 tbsp chat masala (optional)*
◇ *½ tsp sugar*
◇ *Salt to taste*
◇ *Freshly chopped coriander to garnish*

Method

1 If using dry channa, soak them overnight in some warm water and boil them in a pressure cooker the following day.

2 Braise the diced onion until brown.

3 Add the tomatoes and the rest of the ingredients and simmer for 3-5 minutes.

4 Add the cooked channa to this mixture and bring gently to the boil.

5 Taste and adjust for salt.

6 Garnish with chopped coriander and serve with puris or bhaturas.

Fried potatoes

ONE OF THE MOST COMMON AND AUTHENTIC FIRST DISHES AN INDIAN MOTHER MIGHT TEACH HER DAUGHTER TO COOK

Preparation time: 10 minutes
Cooking time: 15 minutes
Serves 4

You will need:

◇ *2-3 medium potatoes, peeled, washed and diced in cubes*
◇ *2 tbsp cooking oil*
◇ *½ tsp mustard seeds*
◇ *1 tsp fresh crushed garlic*
◇ *Salt to taste*
◇ *1 tsp fresh crushed green chillies*
◇ *A pinch of turmeric powder*
◇ *Freshly chopped coriander to garnish*

Method

1 Blanche the diced potatoes in hot boiling water so that they are semi-cooked.

2 Heat oil in a frying pan or wok and add the mustard seeds.

3 When the mustard seeds start to pop, add the garlic and the blanched potatoes.

4 Stir in salt, green chillies and turmeric.

5 Allow to cook for approximately 10 minutes, stirring regularly until the potatoes are crisp and cooked.

6 Serve hot garnished with coriander.

Aloo methi

STUDIES HAVE SHOWN THAT FENUGREEK OR METHI IS A POTENT STIMULATOR OF BREAST MILK PRODUCTION, SO YOUNG MOTHERS ARE OFTEN ENCOURAGED TO EAT THIS DISH

Preparation time: 10 minutes
Cooking time: 15 minutes
Serves 4

You will need:

◇ *2-3 medium potatoes, peeled, washed and diced in cubes*

◇ *2 tbsp cooking oil*
◇ *1 cup finely chopped fenugreek leaves*
◇ *1 tsp fresh crushed garlic*
◇ *Salt to taste*
◇ *1 tsp fresh crushed green chillies*
◇ *A pinch of turmeric powder*
◇ *Freshly chopped coriander to garnish*

Method

1 Blanche the diced potatoes in hot boiling water so that they are semi-cooked.

2 Heat oil in a frying pan or wok and add the chopped fenugreek leaves and garlic and cook for 4-5 minutes until the water has evaporated.

3 Stir in the salt, green chillies, turmeric and the blanched potatoes.

4 Allow to cook for approximately 5 minutes, stirring regularly until the potatoes are crisp.

5 Garnish with fresh coriander and serve hot with roti.

Red kidney beans

KNOWN AS RAJMA, IT'S THE MOST AWESOME SOUL FOOD EATEN WITH RICE

Preparation time: 10 minutes
not including overnight soaking
Cooking time: 40 minutes
Serves 4-6

You will need:

◇ *1 cup red kidney beans*
or 400g can cooked red kidney beans
◇ *2 tbsp cooking oil*

◇ *1 medium onion chopped*
◇ *1 tomato liquidised*
◇ *1 tsp tomato purée*
◇ *1 tsp fresh crushed garlic*
◇ *1 tsp fresh crushed ginger*
◇ *1 tsp fresh crushed green chillies*
or red chilli powder
◇ *1 tsp salt*
◇ *Freshly chopped coriander to garnish*

Method

1 Wash and soak the kidney beans overnight. The following day, boil or pressure cook them in a cup of water and a pinch of salt until they become soft and mushy. (Omit if using canned beans.)

2 Heat some oil in a medium pan and braise the onion until light brown. Add the liquidised tomato and the tomato purée and the rest of the spices and cook until blended.

3 Add the cooked beans, bring to boil, taste and adjust for salt and chilli.

4 Garnish with coriander and serve hot with rice or rotis.

Karela

ALSO KNOWN AS BITTER GOURD, IT'S RICH IN PHOSPHOROUS

Preparation time: 20 minutes
Cooking time: 35 minutes
Serves 4

You will need:

◇ 6 large karelas
◇ 1 tsp turmeric powder
◇ 1 tsp coriander
◇ 1 tsp cumin powder
◇ *1 tsp fresh finely chopped ginger*
◇ *1 tsp fresh finely chopped garlic*
◇ *1 tsp red chillies*
◇ *1 tsp sugar*
◇ *Salt to taste*
◇ *2 tsp cooking oil*
◇ *Oil for frying*
◇ *2 onions sliced long*
◇ *½ tsp garam masala*
◇ *Freshly chopped coriander to garnish*

Method

1 Wash and scrape the outer roughness off the karelas and keep the scrapes to one side.

2 Slit the karelas lengthwise without cutting through. Remove the insides and mix with the outer scrapes.

3 Soak both these mixtures in salty water for 30 minutes and keep to one side.

4 In a separate bowl, mix the turmeric, coriander cumin, ginger, garlic, chillies, sugar, salt and 2 tsp oil. Stuff each karela with this spice mixture, then tie them with thread to keep the mixture intact.

5 Deep fry the karelas until brown all over. When cool remove the threads. In a separate pot, heat some oil and braise the onions.

6 Take the scrapes mixture and rinse thoroughly to remove all the saltiness. Drain and add this to the onions. Cook for approximately 4-5 minutes.

7 Add the fried karelas and cook for 1-2 minutes. Add the garam masala, stir and taste for salt and adjust. Garnish with coriander and serve with roti.

Additionally, you can add potatoes. Cut them lengthwise like chips, fry and add to the onions at the same time as the karelas.

Stuffed bhinda

ALSO KNOWN AS LADY FINGERS, THIS DISH IS BRIMMING WITH FLAVOUR

Preparation time: 10 minutes
Cooking time: 15 minutes
Serves 4

You will need:

◇ *200g bhinda*
◇ *1 tsp salt*
◇ *1 tsp red chilli powder*
◇ *½ tsp turmeric powder*
◇ *1 tbsp garam masala*
◇ *1 sliced onion*
◇ *2-3 tbsp cooking oil*
◇ *½ tsp fresh crushed garlic*
◇ *Freshly chopped coriander to garnish*

Method

1 Soak and wash the bhinda in water and pat them dry.

2 Make a slit in each bhinda across horizontally, so that spices can be stuffed.

3 Prepare the stuffing mixture by mixing together the salt, chillies, turmeric, garam masala into a paste-like consistency.

4 Carefully fill each bhinda with the stuffing mixture and keep aside.

5 Braise the onion in the oil, add the garlic and stir.

6 Add the whole stuffed bhinda.

7 Cover the pan and cook on a low heat until the bhinda is completely cooked.

8 Occasionally – and carefully – turn the bhinda over with a spatula so it cooks on all sides.

9 Garnish with coriander and serve hot with roti.

Eggplant bartha

THIS SMOKED AND MASHED EGGPLANT DISH HAS AN EXOTIC FLAVOUR

Preparation time: 20 minutes
Cooking time: 10 minutes
Serves 4

You will need:

◇ *1 large eggplant*

◇ *1 large onion diced into small cubes*
◇ *1 tbsp fresh crushed garlic*
◇ *1 tbsp fresh crushed green chillies*
◇ *Salt to taste*
◇ *1 tbsp olive oil*
◇ *Freshly chopped coriander to garnish*

Method

1 Roast the large eggplant on a direct flame turning it gently until the skin turns black and brittle.

2 Take it off the flame and allow to cool.

3 Peel off the skin and add the flesh to the rest of the ingredients in a pan and cook on a low heat.

4 Mix well and cook until the flesh is totally mashed and the ingredients are well mixed.

5 Garnish with freshly chopped coriander and serve hot with rotis.

Fresh chopped tomatoes can be added during the cooking process, if preferred. This dish can also be used as a dip that's served with pitta bread.

Paneer

DATING BACK TO ANCIENT INDIA, PANEER IS THE MOST COMMON TYPE OF CHEESE USED IN TRADITIONAL INDIAN CUISINE

Preparation time: 10 minutes using ready-made paneer
Cooking time: 15 minutes
Serves 4

You will need:

◇ 2 cups milk
◇ 2 tbsp white vinegar

Paneer stir fry:

◇ 1 tbsp cooking oil
◇ 1 onion sliced long and thin
◇ 1 each red, green and yellow pepper sliced long and thin
◇ 1 tsp red chilli powder
◇ 1 tsp fresh crushed garlic
◇ 1 tsp tomato purée
◇ 1 tsp salt
◇ 1 tsp chaat masala (optional)
◇ Freshly chopped coriander to garnish

Paneer with peas:

◇ 1 tbsp cooking oil
◇ 1 large onion diced up
◇ 300g fresh peas
◇ 1 tbsp plain yoghurt
◇ 1 tomato diced or 1 tbsp tomato purée
◇ 1 tsp red chilli powder
◇ 1 tsp fresh crushed garlic
◇ 1 tsp salt
◇ Freshly chopped coriander to garnish

Paneer with corn:

◇ 1 tbsp cooking oil
◇ 1 onion diced
◇ 1-2 tomatoes liquidised
◇ 1 tsp salt
◇ 1 tsp red chilli powder
◇ 1 tsp fresh crushed garlic
◇ 1 can sweetcorn or 1 cup of frozen corn
◇ Freshly chopped coriander to garnish

Method for paneer

1 To make the paneer, boil the milk and add the vinegar while the milk is boiling. This will curdle the milk.

2 Place the curdled milk onto the muslin cloth to drain off the water.

3 Hang this cloth over the sink for a few hours to make sure the water is completely drained.

4 Place a heavy item like a big book on the cloth to flatten and harden the paneer.

5 To make the fried paneer cut the paneer into cubes and shallow fry until slightly brown in colour. Alternatively if using ready-made paneer, cut into cubes and soak in hot water for 1-2 minutes. Drain and shallow fry until golden brown.

Chef's tip

Homemade paneer has a fresh quality to it and a dense, crumbly texture that works beautifully with strong flavours.

Method for stir fry paneer

1 Heat 1 tbsp oil and add the onions and peppers. Gently stir fry.

2 Add the chillies, garlic and the tomato purée.

3 Add salt to taste and cook for 2-3 minutes. Once the veggies are crisp add the fried paneer cubes and continue to stir fry for 1-2 minutes.

4 Add chopped coriander to garnish and some chaat masala (optional). This can be served as a starter or with a main meal.

Method for paneer with peas

1 Heat 1 tbsp oil and braise the onion. Add the peas and let them cook. Add the yoghurt, tomato purée, chillies and the garlic. Add salt to taste and simmer for 2-3 minutes.

2 Add the shallow fried paneer and stir. Simmer with ½ cup of water.

3 Serve garnished with chopped coriander.

Method for paneer with corn

1 Heat 1 tbsp oil and braise the onion. Add the liquidised tomatoes, salt, chillies, garlic and cook for 5 minutes.

2 Add the corn and stir. Finally add the fried paneer and stir well. Cook for 5 minutes.

3 Garnish with chopped coriander and serve as a starter or with a main meal.

Sekta-ni-sing

KNOWN AS THE DRUMSTICK BEAN, THIS IS A GREEN VEGETABLE IN A LONG STICK-LIKE POD. THE OUTER POD IS NOT EDIBLE. THE ONLY EDIBLE PARTS ARE THE BEANS INSIDE, AND THEY ARE A RARE DELICACY

Preparation time: 10 minutes
Cooking time: 20 minutes
Serves 4

You will need:

◇ *1 bunch of sekta-ni-sing (drumsticks)*
◇ *1 tbsp cooking oil*
◇ *½ cup gram flour*
◇ *1 tsp fresh crushed garlic*
◇ *1 tsp salt*
◇ *A pinch of turmeric powder*
◇ *1 tsp red chilli powder*
◇ *Freshly chopped coriander to garnish*

Method

1 Scrape the drumsticks, then cut them into long pieces and wash well.

2 Boil these in hot water with a pinch of salt. Avoid over boiling as the drumsticks may start to break.

3 Heat the oil in a pan, add the gram flour and roast until it changes colour.

4 Add the garlic, salt, turmeric and the chilli powder and cook on a low heat. Excessively high heat will burn the gram flour very quickly so stick to low heat until the fragrance is out.

5 Add a bit more oil if required – this varies with different gram flours.

6 Add the boiled drumsticks. Add about ½ cup water and let it cook until the gravy thickens. Adjust for salt.

7 Garnish with coriander and serve hot.

White haricot beans

A RELATIVE OF THE BAKED BEAN FAMILY, THESE ARE PACKED WITH PROTEIN

Preparation time: 10 minutes
not including overnight soaking
Cooking time: 20 minutes
Serves 4

You will need:

◇ 1 cup white haricot beans or
400g can cooked haricot beans
◇ 1 tsp salt
◇ 2 tbsp cooking oil
◇ ½ tsp carom seeds
◇ 1 tsp fresh crushed garlic
◇ 1 tsp sesame seeds
◇ 2 tomatoes liquidised
◇ 1 tsp red chilli powder
◇ ½ tsp sugar
◇ 2 tbsp plain yoghurt
◇ Freshly chopped coriander to garnish

Method

1 Soak the beans overnight in warm water.

2 The following day, clean and pressure-cook them in 1 cup hot water with a pinch of salt. To ensure they're cooked, place a bean between your fingers and test how hard it feels when pressed. It requires more boiling if it's still hard. (Alternatively, you can use a can of cooked haricot beans.)

3 In a separate pot, heat the oil, add the carom seeds and garlic. Stir well. Add the sesame seeds and cover with lid to stop the sesame seeds from popping out.

4 Add the liquidised tomatoes. Add salt, chillies and sugar. Simmer for 4-5 minutes until cooked.

5 Meanwhile, pour the yoghurt into a blender with the coriander and liquidise for a minute. Add this to the cooked white beans. Add the beans and yoghurt mixture to the cooked tomato sauce and let it boil. Taste for salt and adjust.

6 Garnish with coriander and serve hot with boiled rice or roti.

Stuffed green peppers

THIS IS A DISH WHICH EXISTS IN DIFFERENT FORMS AROUND THE WORLD

Preparation time: 10 minutes
Cooking time: 15 minutes
Serves 4

You will need:

◇ 4-5 medium green peppers
◇ 1 cup gram flour
◇ 3 tbsp cooking oil
◇ 1 tsp salt
◇ 1 tsp red chilli powder
◇ 1 tsp fresh crushed garlic
◇ A pinch of sugar
◇ 1 tbsp ground peanuts (optional)
◇ Freshly chopped coriander to garnish

Method

1 Wash and cut the peppers in half so they form a cup shape. Remove the seeds and the pulp and keep the empty pepper shells to one side.

2 Roast the gram flour in 2 tbsp oil on a low heat. Stir until the colour changes. Add the spices and peanuts if desired. Stir well. Taste and adjust. Divide this mixture into the green pepper cups.

3 Heat 1 tbsp oil in a separate pan and place the peppers in it, spread apart.

4 Cover and let them simmer. They should cook in their own juices but check frequently and add a small amount of water if the mixture is too dry. Garnish with coriander and serve.

Sprouted moong

THESE HEALTHY SPROUTS ARE A GREAT ADDITION TO WRAPS AND SALADS

Sprouting time: About 2 days
Cooking time: 15 minutes
Serves 2-4

You will need:

◇ *1 cup whole moong or*
1-1½ cups ready sprouted moong
◇ *2 tbsp cooking oil*
◇ *1 tsp cumin seeds*

◇ *1 onion chopped*
◇ *1 tsp cumin powder*
◇ *1 tsp coriander powder*
◇ *1 tsp garam masala*
◇ *1 tsp fresh crushed garlic*
◇ *1 tsp fresh crushed ginger*
◇ *1 tsp red chilli powder*
◇ *Salt to taste*
◇ *1 tsp fresh crushed green chillies*
◇ *½ cup hot water*

Method

1 To sprout the moong, wash well and soak them in warm water overnight.

2 The folllowing day, wash and drain all the water from the moong. Place the soaked moong in a damp muslin cloth or a thin dish towel. Tie the cloth and leave inside a colander.

3 Cover and keep in a warm, dark place away from drafts. (Placing it in an oven in the off position works well, too.) Leave the moong for 2 days checking on it occasionally in case it sprouts sooner. If the cloth seems to have dried up, lightly sprinkle with water to re-moisten.

4 Wash the sprouts several times to remove the loose skins while retaining the sprouts. (If using ready sprouted moong, omit steps 1-3.)

5 Heat the oil in a pot and add the cumin seeds. When the seeds start to pop, add the onion and cook for 1-2 minutes. Add the rest of the ingredients except the water. Cover and cook for 5 minutes.

6 Add the sprouted moong and mix well. Add ½ cup water, cover and allow to steam-cook. Do not overcook as this will make the moong go mushy. Leave on a medium heat for 15 minutes. Garnish with coriander and serve hot with roti.

Lentils are friendly
– the Miss Congeniality
of the bean world

LAURIE COLWIN

DAHLS

Chevti dahl

THIS IS A MIXTURE OF LENTILS. IT IS CHOLESTEROL-FREE, A GREAT
SOURCE OF SODIUM AND POTASSIUM AND LOW IN FAT AND CARBS.
A WONDERFUL, WHOLESOME DISH – ESPECIALLY IN WINTER

Preparation time: 10 minutes
Cooking time: 20 minutes
Serves 4-6

You will need:

◇ ¼ cup toor dahl
◇ ¼ cup channa dahl
◇ ½ cup split urad dahl (white)

◇ *1 cup water*
◇ *2 tbsp cooking oil*
◇ *A pinch of cumin seeds*
◇ *1 tsp fresh crushed garlic*
◇ *1 tsp red chilli powder*
◇ *1 tsp salt*
◇ *A pinch of turmeric powder*
◇ *1 large tomato liquidised*
◇ *Freshly chopped coriander to garnish*

Method

1 Mix the three dahls together and wash well.

2 Add 1 cup water to this and boil in a pressure cooker for about 10 minutes. When cooked,
the dahl should appear pale yellow in colour and all the grains of the dahls should be blended.

3 Heat the oil and add the cumin seeds. When these begin to pop add the garlic. Add the
chilli powder, salt, turmeric powder and the liquidised tomato and simmer for 4-5 minutes.

4 Add the cooked dahl and bring to the boil on a slow heat.

5 Taste and adjust salt.

6 Garnish with chopped coriander and serve hot with rotis.

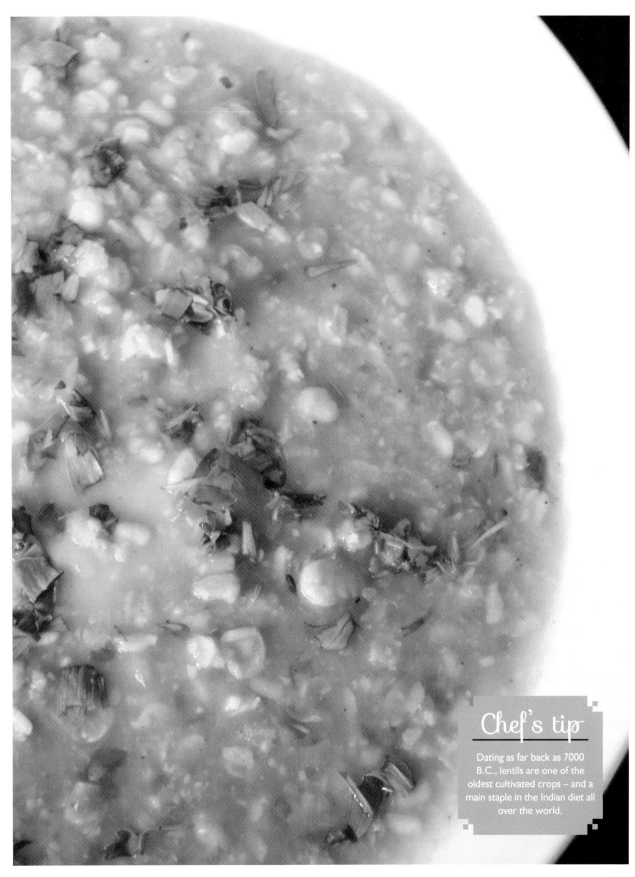

Gujarati kadhi

A SOOTHING DISH IN WINTER MONTHS, IT HELPS RELIEVE SORE THROATS

Preparation time: 10 minutes
Cooking time: 10 minutes
Serves 3-4

You will need:

◇ *1 cup plain yoghurt*
◇ *2 tbsp gram flour*
◇ *1 tsp fresh crushed garlic*
◇ *1 tsp fresh crushed green chillies*
◇ *1 tsp salt*
◇ *1 tbsp crushed green peas (optional)*
◇ *A pinch of citric acid (optional)*
◇ *A pinch of sugar*
◇ *½ cup water*
◇ *A few curry leaves*
◇ *Freshly chopped coriander to garnish*

For the tadka:

◇ *1 tsp cumin seeds*
◇ *1 tbsp cooking oil or ghee*

Method

1 Blend the yoghurt, gram flour, garlic, green chillies, salt, peas, citric acid powder, sugar and water in an electric blender.

2 Taste and adjust for salt and sourness. Taste, and if it's too sour, add a pinch of sugar and if it's not quite sour enough, add a pinch of citric acid.

3 For the tadka, roast cumin seeds until they blacken.

4 Turn off the heat, add the oil or ghee.

5 Add the blended yoghurt mixture and curry leaves to this and bring to the boil, stirring all the time.

6 Garnish with chopped coriander and serve hot.

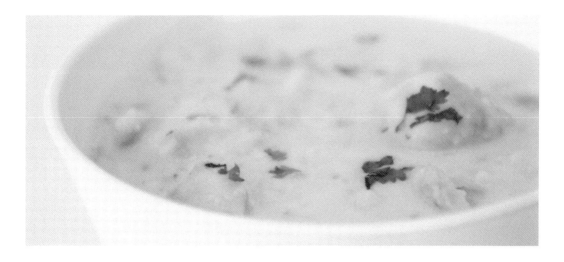

Punjabi kadhi

THIS IS A MORE SUBSTANTIAL MEAL COMPARED TO THE GUJARATI VERSION

Preparation time: 15 minutes
Cooking time: 10 minutes
Serves 3-4

For the bhajias:

◇ 1 cup gram flour
◇ 1 tsp salt
◇ 1 tsp red chilli powder
◇ 1 tsp fresh crushed garlic
◇ 1 onion sliced (optional)
◇ 1 tsp cooking oil
◇ ½ cup water
◇ Cooking oil to fry

For the kadhi:

◇ 1 cup plain yoghurt
◇ 2 tbsp gram flour
◇ ½ tsp turmeric
◇ 1 tsp fresh crushed green chillies
◇ 1 tsp fresh crushed garlic
◇ 1 tsp salt
◇ A pinch of citric acid (optional)
◇ A pinch of sugar
◇ ½ cup water
◇ Freshly chopped coriander to garnish

For the tadka:

◇ 1 tsp cumin seeds
◇ 1 tbsp cooking oil or ghee
◇ A few curry leaves

Method

1 For the bhajias, mix all the ingredients to a thick paste. Using 1 tbsp of the mixture at a time, deep fry into circles in medium hot oil. Keep these bhajias aside.

2 Blend all the kadhi ingredients in an electric blender.

3 Taste and adjust for salt and sourness – add a pinch of sugar if it's too sour, or citric acid if it's not quite sour enough.

4 For the tadka, roast the cumin seeds until they blacken. Turn off the heat, add the oil or ghee and add the blended yoghurt/kadhi mixture and the curry leaves, stirring all the time.

5 Put it back on the heat and add the bhajias. Let it boil. The bhajias will absorb the kadhi and swell in size. Add a little more water if the kadhi is too thick in consistency.

6 Garnish with chopped coriander and serve hot.

Sweetcorn kadhi

THIS FAMILY FAVOURITE OF MINE MAKES A SCRUMPTIOUS EVENING MEAL

Preparation time: 10 minutes
Cooking time: 15 minutes
Serves 3-4

You will need:

◇ 2 whole kernels of sweetcorn
or 3-4 pieces of frozen corn on cob
◇ 2 tbsp cooking oil or ghee
◇ 2 tbsp gram flour
◇ 1 cup plain yoghurt
◇ 1 tsp fresh crushed green chillies
◇ 1 tsp salt
◇ 1 tsp freshly crushed garlic
◇ A few curry leaves
◇ Citric acid (optional)
◇ Freshly chopped coriander to garnish
◇ A pinch of sugar to taste

For the tadka:

◇ 1 tsp cumin seeds
◇ 1 tbsp cooking oil or ghee

Method

1 Cut the cobs into bite-size pieces, wash and boil until cooked.

2 Heat the oil in a pan, add the gram flour and stir continuously until the flour starts to turn brown.

3 Take off the heat. Using an electric blender or whisk mix the yoghurt, chillies, salt, garlic, curry leaves, and coriander. Taste, if it's too sour, add a pinch of sugar. If it's not sour enough, add citric acid.

4 Pour this blended mixture over the brown gram flour, again, mixing continuously.

5 Boil the mixture to an even consistency stirring all the time. Add the boiled corn cobs. Bring this to boil so that it thickens.

6 For the tadka, roast cumin seeds until they blacken. Take off heat and add the oil or ghee. Add this oil to the yoghurt and sweetcorn mixture. Stir and allow to boil.

7 Garnish with chopped coriander and serve it hot with rice.

Moong dahl

IN HINDU CULTURE MONDAY IS DEDICATED TO LORD SHIVA AND MOONG IS MADE AS AN OFFERING. MANY HINDUS FAST ON MONDAYS AND THIS DAHL IS ON THE MENU ON THE DAY

Preparation time: 20 minutes
Cooking time: 25 minutes
Serves 2-4

You will need:

◇ *1 cup moong*
◇ *2 tbsp toor dahl*
◇ *1 tbsp cooking oil*
◇ *½ tsp mustard seeds*
◇ *A few curry leaves*
◇ *1 tsp fresh crushed garlic*
◇ *2 tomatoes liquidised*
◇ *1 tsp salt*
◇ *½ tsp turmeric powder*
◇ *1 whole dried red chilli (optional)*
◇ *Freshly chopped coriander to garnish*

Method

1 Mix together the moong and the toor dahl. Wash and soak for 10 minutes.

2 Drain and cook the dahl in 1 cup water in a pressure cooker, with a pinch of salt for 20 minutes. Alternatively, boil it in a pot until it goes soft and mushy. This may take up to an hour.

3 Heat the oil in a pot and add the mustard seeds, curry leaves and garlic. When the seeds start to pop add the tomatoes, salt, chilli, turmeric and the whole dried red chilli. Cook gently until blended.

4 Add the cooked moong and bring it to boil. Taste and adjust.

5 Garnish with chopped coriander and serve hot with rotis or boiled rice.

Dahl makhani

THE BLACK SKIN OF THE URAD DAHL DISGUISES A CREAMY WHITE CENTRE
THAT IS RICH IN ESSENTIAL IRON

Preparation time: 10 minutes
plus soaking overnight
Cooking time: 30-40 minutes
Serves 4-6

You will need:

◇ *1 cup whole urad dahl (black)*
◇ *1 tbsp red kidney beans*
◇ *1 tsp salt*

◇ *2 tbsp cooking oil*
◇ *1 large onion diced*
◇ *1 tsp fresh crushed garlic*
◇ *1 tbsp fresh crushed ginger*
◇ *2 tomatoes liquidised*
or 400g can peeled tomatoes
◇ *1 tsp red chilli powder*
◇ *2 tbsp fresh cream*
◇ *Freshly chopped coriander to garnish*

Method

1 Soak the mixture of dahl and the red kidney beans in two cups of hot water overnight. The following day, wash well and cook in a pressure cooker with 1½ cups water and salt. Let it cook for 20 minutes.

2 Meanwhile heat 1 tbsp oil in a pan and braise the onion until it goes brown.

3 Add the garlic and ginger and stir well. Add the tomatoes and chilli and simmer for 10 minutes.

4 The cooked dahl should be soft and almost mushy. Add this to the tomato mixture and stir well. Bring it to the boil on a slow heat. Taste and adjust accordingly for salt.

5 Add the fresh cream and keep stirring until it blends in over a very low heat.

6 Garnish with coriander and serve with rotis and an onion and tomato salad.

Toor dahl

A STAPLE FOOD IN GUJARATI HOMES, ALSO KNOWN AS SPLIT PIGEON PEAS

Preparation time: 15 minutes
Cooking time: 25 minutes
Serves 3-4

◇ *1 tbsp tamarind water (optional)*
◇ *A pinch of citric acid*
◇ *¼ tsp sugar*
◇ *Freshly chopped coriander to garnish*

You will need:

◇ *1 cup toor dahl*
◇ *1 medium tomato cut into quarters*
◇ *2 tbsp ground nuts (optional)*
◇ *1 tsp salt*
◇ *1 tsp red chillies or fresh green chillies*
◇ *1 tsp fresh crushed garlic*

For the tadka:

◇ *1 tbsp cooking oil*
◇ *¼ tsp mustard seeds*
◇ *¼ tsp fenugreek seeds*
◇ *2-3 cloves*
◇ *A few curry leaves*
◇ *1 whole red dried chilli (optional)*

Method

1 Soak the dahl in a cup of warm water for about 10 minutes and wash thoroughly.

2 Using a pressure cooker, boil the dahl with the tomatoes and salt in a little more than a cup of water. Boil for 20 minutes on a medium heat. Boil the groundnuts separately until cooked. Put aside.

3 Sieve the dahl to remove tomato peels and dahl grains. The dahl should be an even consistency. Add chillies, garlic, tamarind water, citric acid, sugar and coriander. Mix, and add the groundnuts.

4 For the tadka, heat 1 tbsp oil in a pan. When hot, add mustard, fenugreek, cloves, curry leaves, red chilli.

5 When the seeds start to pop, add the dahl mixture and bring it to boil. If the consistency is too thick, add water. Taste, and adjust salt accordingly. Garnish with fresh coriander and serve hot with rice.

To a man with
an empty stomach,
food is gold

MAHATMA GANDHI

BREADS

Aloo paratha

EXTREMELY POPULAR WITH NORTH INDIANS, THESE ARE BEST EATEN WITH CHILLED YOGHURT AND YOUR FAVORITE PICKLE OR CHUTNEY

Preparation time: 15 minutes
Cooking time: 10 minutes
Serves 4

You will need:

◇ *2 medium potatoes*
◇ *1 tsp salt*
◇ *1 tsp red chilli powder*
◇ *Freshly chopped coriander*
◇ *1 tsp dried crushed pomegranate seeds (optional)*
◇ *1 onion diced (optional)*
◇ *Dough as per plain paratha, but softer, see page 89*
◇ *Cooking oil or ghee*

Method

1 Wash and boil the potatoes. Peel and mash them once cooked.

2 Add the salt, chilli and coriander to the mashed potatoes and add crushed dried pomegranate seeds and onions, if desired.

3 Mix well and allow to cool before rolling out the parathas.

4 Make the plain paratha dough and soften it with some water. It should be as soft as the mashed potato. Divide the dough into small balls, roll each ball to about 8cm in diameter, tossing in dry flour.

5 Make a small ball of the spiced mashed potatoes (approximately the size of a golf ball), and place it in the centre of the rolled dough.

6 Pull and pinch the dough over the mashed potato ball to make a bigger ball with the dough on the outside and the mashed potato on the inside.

7 Toss the bigger ball in dry flour and roll to about 12-15cm in diameter. If the potato filling spreads out then either there is too much potato or the dough is too soft or you are using too much pressure when rolling.

8 Heat a frying pan to medium heat. Place the rolled paratha onto the pan and roast for 1-2 minutes.

9 Add 1 tsp oil or butter around the perimeter of the paratha. Flip over to cook the other side adding a little more oil around the perimeter. Flip again and cook until golden brown. Repeat the process with the rest of the dough. Serve hot.

Chef's tip

Parathas are wholewheat
Indian flatbread. They can be
made plain or stuffed with
many different fillings. This
recipe uses the most popular
filling – potatoes. Aloo parathas
are perfect for a weekend
breakfast or brunch.

Roti

PEOPLE FROM ALL REGIONS IN INDIA EAT ROTI (ROTLI, PHULKA), AN UNLEAVENED BREAD. SERVE IT FRESH AND HOT WITH ANY CURRY DISH

Preparation time: 10 minutes
Cooking time: 5 minutes
Serves 4-6

You will need:

◇ ¾ cup warm water
◇ 1½ cups wheat flour
◇ 1 tsp cooking oil or ghee
◇ Butter or ghee for dabbing (optional)

Method

1 Boil the warm water. Place the flour in a bowl and oil or ghee. Rub this into the flour.

2 Add half the water to make a soft dough, adding more water as required.

3 Knead well with oiled hands to make a smooth, soft dough. Divide into small balls. Take each ball and flatten it, then toss in dry wheat flour. Roll it into a thin circle about 12-14cm in diameter.

4 Heat a frying pan to medium heat. Place the rolled roti in the pan and roast until small freckles start to appear. Turn over and press gently with a cloth while turning and allow it to puff up. (Alternatively, you can place the roti directly on the flame or the burner, turning over several times until lightly freckled.)

5 The well-burned roti is the one with a light background with gold brown freckles dotted evenly.

6 Remove the roti from the pan and transfer to a serving dish. Brush with butter or ghee, if desired. Repeat with the remaining dough. Serve hot.

Plain paratha

THESE CAN BE FUN AS YOU
CAN ROLL THEM INTO ROUND,
SQUARE OR TRIANGLE SHAPES
– OR INDEED, ANY OTHER!

Preparation time:
5 minutes
Cooking time:
15 minutes
Serves 4

You will need:
◇ *Cooking oil or ghee*
◇ *2 cups wheat flour*
◇ *Warm water*

Method

1 Rub 1 tbsp oil with the flour and bind the dough with warm water to a firm consistency.

2 Divide this into 8-9 balls. Toss each ball in dry flour and roll each ball into a small circle approximately 6-8cm in diameter. Spread about ½ tsp oil or ghee onto the dough circles.

3 Bring the top edge of the rolled circle to the centre and repeat with the bottom edge. Fold the remaining edges of the circle to the middle overlapping to form a square shape. Roll this out into a bigger square about 15cm square.

4 Heat a frying pan to medium heat. Place the rolled paratha onto the pan and roast for 1-2 minutes.

5 Add 1 tsp oil or butter around the perimeter of the paratha. Flip over to cook the other side adding a little more oil around the perimeter. Flip again and cook until golden brown. Repeat the process with the rest of the balls.

6 Serve hot with an Indian omelette for breakfast or serve with any vegetable or meat curries. It can also be served as a snack with mango or lime pickle.

Mooli paratha

WHITE RADISH IS A PUNJABI FAVORITE

Preparation time:
15 minutes
Cooking time:
10 minutes
Serves 4-5

You will need:
◇ *1 large mooli*
◇ *1-2 tsp salt*
◇ *1-2 tsp red chilli powder*
◇ *Freshly chopped coriander*
◇ *Dough as per plain paratha, see opposite*
◇ *Cooking oil or ghee*

Method

1 Peel, wash and grate the radish. Leave the grated radish in a muslin cloth to drain.

2 Radish gives out a lot of water, making it hard to roll. This can cause the paratha to break. To prevent this, only add salt, chilli and coriander just before preparing the parathas. Squeeze, each time you fill the paratha before rolling out.

3 Make the plain paratha dough and soften with water. Divide into small balls. Toss each ball in dry flour and roll into a circle approximately 6-8cm in diameter.

4 Place 1 tbsp radish onto the centre of the rolled dough. Pull and pinch the dough over the radish to make a bigger ball with the dough on the outside and the radish on the inside.

5 Toss this bigger ball in dry flour and roll to about 12-15cm in diameter. Heat a frying pan to medium heat. Place the rolled paratha in the pan and roast for 1-2 minutes.

6 Add 1 tsp oil or ghee around the perimeter of the paratha. Flip to cook the other side adding more oil. Flip again and cook until golden brown. Repeat with the remainder. Serve.

Gobi paratha

CAULIFLOWER MAKES A TASTY FILLING

Preparation time:
15 minutes
Cooking time:
10 minutes
Serves 4

You will need:

◇ *1 small cauliflower*
◇ *Salt to taste*
◇ *1 tsp red chilli powder*
◇ *Chopped coriander*
◇ *Dough as per plain paratha, see page 89*
◇ *Cooking oil or ghee*

Method

1 Wash and cut the gobi (cauliflower) in small florets. Blanche by placing in a metal sieve and dipping in hot boiling water for 1-2 minutes. When cool add salt, chilli and coriander.

2 Make the plain paratha dough and soften with water. Divide the dough into small balls, roll each one tossing in dry flour to a circle, 8cm in diameter.

3 Place 1 tbsp cauliflower onto the centre of the rolled dough. Pull and pinch the dough over the cauliflower to make a bigger ball with the dough on the outside and the cauliflower on the inside.

4 Toss the bigger ball in dry flour and roll to about 12-15cm in diameter.

5 Heat a frying pan to medium heat. Place the paratha onto the pan and roast for 1-2 minutes.

6 Add 1 tsp oil or butter around the perimeter of the paratha. Flip over to cook the other side adding a little more oil around the perimeter. Flip again and cook until golden brown. Repeat the process with the rest of the ball. Serve with yoghurt and tomato and onion salad.

Paneer paratha can be made by grating paneer. Add salt, chilli powder and coriander and roll using paneer only or a paneer/cauliflower mix.

Poora

A HEALTHY INDIAN SPICED SAVOURY PANCAKE-LIKE MEAL. A QUICK DISH WHICH YOU CAN ENJOY ON THE GO

Preparation time: 10 minutes
Cooking time: 10 minutes
Serves 4

You will need:

◇ *½ cup gram flour*
◇ *½ cup wheat flour*
◇ *1 tsp salt*
◇ *½ tsp chopped fresh garlic*
◇ *1 tsp red chilli powder*
◇ *4-6 tbsp fresh washed and chopped fenugreek leaves (methi)*
◇ *8-10 tbsp butter milk (mixture of half warm water and half plain yoghurt)*
◇ *Cooking oil to fry*

Method

1 Sift the two flours together and add the spices and fenugreek leaves.

2 Gradually add the butter milk to form a fairly smooth batter.

3 Heat a non-stick pan on low heat, grease it evenly with some oil and pour ¼ ladle cup of the batter into the pan and spread it to a thin round shape.

4 Pour a little oil around the perimeter of the batter and when the underside turns a golden brown. Turn over the poora.

5 Remove from the pan when both sides are golden brown.

6 Serve it hot with coriander chutney and some plain yoghurt.

Semolina pooras

SEMOLINA IS OFTEN USED AS AN INGREDIENT TO MAKE INDIAN BREADS AS IT TENDS TO ABSORB MOISTURE

Preparation time: 10 minutes
Cooking time: 10 minutes
Serves 4

You will need:

◇ *1 cup fine semolina*
◇ *½ cup plain yoghurt*
◇ *1 small finely chopped onion*
◇ *1 tsp freshly chopped ginger*
◇ *1 tsp crushed fresh garlic*
◇ *1 tsp chopped green chilies*
◇ *½ tsp salt*
◇ *½ cup water*
◇ *Oil for greasing*

Method

1 Mix all the ingredients except the water and the oil in a large bowl.

2 Add small amount of water at a time to make the batter.

3 Heat a non-stick pan on low heat, grease it evenly with some oil and, when hot, pour ¼ ladle cup of batter into the pan and spread it to a thin round shape.

4 Pour a little oil around the perimeter of the batter and when the underside turns a golden brown turn over the poora.

5 Remove from the pan when both sides are golden brown.

6 Serve it hot with coriander chutney and plain yoghurt.

For variation, you can add 1 tbsp gram flour or fresh chopped fenugreek leaves or chopped spinach.

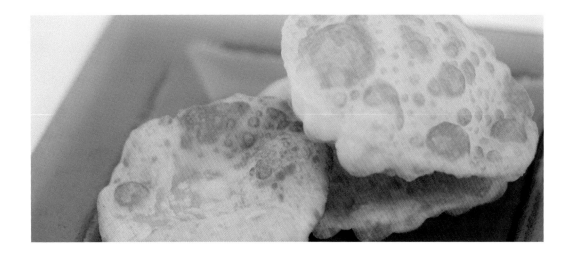

Bhatura

TASTY, FRIED INDIAN BREAD, OFTEN EATEN WITH CHANNA (CHICKPEAS)

Preparation time: 2-3 hours including storing time for the dough
Cooking time: 20-30 minutes
Serves 4-6

You will need:

◇ 2 tsp oil
◇ 2 cups cake flour
◇ 1 tsp baking powder
◇ 1 tsp salt
◇ 1 tsp sugar
◇ 2 tbsp plain yoghurt
◇ ¾ cup warm water or ¼ cup soda water mixed with ½ cup water
◇ Cooking oil to fry

Method

1 Rub the oil into the cake flour and add baking powder, salt, sugar and yoghurt. Mix well.

2 Using the warm water or the soda water mix, a small amount at a time make a soft dough. Knead well and cover with a cloth and keep in a warm place for approximately 2-3hrs.

3 Knead well with a bit of oil on your hands.

4 Divide the dough into small balls. Toss each ball in oil and roll out into a circle approximately 10cm in diameter and repeat with the remaining balls.

5 Deep fry a few at a time in hot oil. To check if the oil is hot enough, drop a small amount of dough into the hot oil and if it sizzles and floats to the surface immediately, then the oil is at the correct temperature for frying. Take the rolled dough and gently slide it from the side of the pan into the hot oil. After a few seconds press it gently using a slotted ladle and flick hot oil onto it. This enhances it to puff up completely.

6 Turn to the other side and fry until golden brown. Remove and place in a colander lined with paper towel. Repeat with the rest of the dough. Serve hot.

Thepla

THESE ARE AN INHERENT PART OF GUJARATI MEALS, AND ARE EATEN AT HOME – OR ON THE ROAD!

Preparation time: 10 minutes
Cooking time: 10 minutes
Serves 4

You will need:

◇ 1 cup wheat flour
◇ 1 tsp fresh crushed green chillies
◇ 1 tsp salt
◇ ½ tsp turmeric
◇ ½ tsp red chilli powder
◇ 1 tsp fresh crushed ginger
◇ 1 tsp fresh crushed garlic
◇ ½ cup washed and chopped fresh fenugreek leaves
◇ Freshly chopped coriander
◇ Warm water to bind
◇ Cooking oil

Method

1 Mix all ingredients with 1tsp of oil, bar the water.

2 Using warm water bind the dough. Knead well with oiled hands to make a smoother soft dough.

3 Divide into small balls. Take each ball and flatten it and toss dry wheat flour and roll into a thin circle approximately 12-14cm in diameter.

4 Heat a frying pan to medium heat. Place the rolled thepla onto the pan and roast for 1-2 minutes.

5 Add 1 tsp oil or butter around the perimeter of the thepla. Flip over to cook the other side adding a little more oil around the perimeter. Flip again and cook until golden brown. Repeat the process with the rest of the balls.

6 Remove from pan and serve with plain yoghurt and mango pickle. Alternatively you can also add leftover boiled rice in the dough.

Naan

BEST COOKED IN A TANDOOR, BUT COOKED ON A PAN IS A GREAT OPTION FOR SPECIAL OCCASIONS

Preparation time: 2-3 hours including storing time for the dough
Cooking time: 20-30 minutes
Serves 4-6

You will need:

◇ 2 tsp cooking oil
◇ 2 cups cake flour
◇ 1 tsp salt
◇ 1 tsp sugar
◇ 2 tbsp plain yoghurt
◇ ¾ cup warm water or ¼ cup soda water mixed with ½ cup water

Method

1 Rub the oil into the cake flour and add the salt, sugar and yoghurt. Mix well.

2 Using the warm water or the soda water mix, a small amount at a time make a soft dough. Knead well and cover with a cloth and keep in a warm place for approximately 2-3hrs.

3 Divide the dough into small balls and roll each ball tossing in dry flour, to an oval shape about 5mm in thickness.

4 Heat a frying pan to medium heat. Place the rolled naan onto the pan and roast until small freckles start to appear. Turn over and press gently with a cloth while turning and allow it to puff up.

5 Alternatively, you can place the naan directly onto the flame or the burner turning over several times until lightly freckled.

6 Remove the naan from the pan and transfer it to a serving dish and brush with butter or ghee if desired.

7 Repeat with the rest of the dough and serve hot.

Plain puri

THIS STYLE OF FRIED BREAD IS FAMOUS IN INDIA WHERE IT'S ENJOYED AT MEALTIMES BY ALL AGE GROUPS

Preparation time:
15 minutes
Cooking time:
10 minutes
Serves 4-6

You will need:

◇ 1 cup wheat (roti) flour
◇ 2 tbsp semolina
◇ 1 tsp salt
◇ 1 tbsp oil
◇ ½ cup warm water
◇ Cooking oil to fry

Method

1 Mix the flour, semolina and salt. Rub in the oil. Using a small amount of water at a time, make the dough.

2 Knead well with a bit of oil on your hands. Divide the dough into small balls and roll out each ball into a circle of approximately 5-6cm in diameter.

3 Deep fry a few at a time in hot oil. To check if the oil is hot enough, drop a small amount of dough into the hot oil and if it sizzles and floats to the surface immediately, then the oil is at the correct temperature for frying. Take the rolled dough and gently slide it from the side of the pan into the hot oil. After a few seconds press it gently using a slotted ladle and flick hot oil onto it. This enhances it to puff up completely.

4 Turn over to the other side and fry until golden brown.

5 Remove and place in a colander lined with paper towel. Repeat with the rest of the dough.

6 Serve hot.

Naan puri

NAAN IS A FLATBREAD ROASTED ON A GRIDDLE. PURI IS FIRED, SO NAAN PURI IS A FUSION OF THE TWO

Preparation time:
10 minutes
Cooking time:
20 minutes
Serves 6

You will need:

◇ 2 cups cake flour
◇ 4 tsp baking powder
◇ ½ tsp salt
◇ 1 tsp sugar
◇ 2 tbsp oil
◇ 1 egg
◇ ¼ cup water mixed with ¼ cup milk
◇ Sesame seeds
◇ Cooking oil to fry

Method

1 Mix the cake flour with the baking powder and add the salt and sugar. Mix well.

2 Add the oil and the egg (keeping some of the egg aside to brush the top of the puri) and make a soft dough using water and milk mixture. Knead well with a bit of oil on your hands. Divide the dough into small balls and roll out each ball into a circle of approximately 5-6cm in diameter.

3 Brush each rolled dough with egg and sprinkle with sesame seeds.

4 Deep fry a few at a time in hot oil. To check if the oil is hot enough, drop a small amount of dough into the hot oil and if it sizzles and floats to the surface immediately, then the oil is at the correct temperature for frying. Take the rolled dough and gently slide it from the side of the pan into the hot oil. After a few seconds press it gently using a slotted ladle and flick hot oil onto it. This enhances it to puff up completely.

5 Turn to the other side and fry until golden brown.

6 Remove and place in a colander lined with paper towel. Repeat with the rest of the dough.

Thiki puri

ROLLED PURI, IF PRICKED BEFORE FRYING, BECOMES REALLY CRISP AND
MAKES A GREAT SNACK. IT WILL ALSO KEEP LONGER

Preparation time: 15 minutes
Cooking time: 10-15 minutes
Serves 6-8

You will need

◇ *1 cup wheat flour*
◇ *2 tbsp semolina*
◇ *1 tbsp oil*
◇ *1 tsp salt*
◇ *1 tsp fresh crushed green chillies*
◇ *1 tsp puri masala (half cumin half carom seeds ground together)*
◇ *½ tsp turmeric (turmeric powder)*
◇ *½ cup warm water*
◇ *Cooking oil to fry*

Method

1 Mix all the flour and the semolina and rub in the oil. Add salt, green chillies, puri masala, turmeric and mix.

2 Add small amount of water at a time to make the dough. Knead into a firm dough.

3 Knead again with a bit of oil on your hands. Divide dough into small balls and roll out each ball into a circle of around 5-6cm in diameter.

4 Deep fry a few at a time in hot oil. To check if the oil is hot enough, drop a small amount of dough into the hot oil and if it sizzles and floats to the surface immediately, then the oil is at the correct temperature for frying. Take the rolled dough and gently slide it from the side of the pan into the hot oil. After a few seconds press it gently using a slotted ladle and flick hot oil onto it. This enhances it to puff up completely.

5 Turn to the other side and fry until golden brown.

6 Remove and place in a colander lined with paper towel. Repeat with the rest of the dough.

7 Serve hot with plain yoghurt and fried papadums.

There is no love
sincerer than the
love of food

GEORGE BERNARD SHAW

RICE
··············

Basic biryani

A WORLD-RENOWNED INDIAN DISH USING FISH, MEAT OR VEGETABLES

Preparation time: 30 minutes
Cooking time: 40 minutes
Serves 4

You will need:

◇ *4 small potatoes*
◇ *Cooking oil*
◇ *2 large onions*
◇ *2 cups rice (Basmati)*
◇ *¼ tsp saffron*
◇ *1½ cups plain yoghurt*
◇ *1 tbsp cumin seeds*
◇ *2 cinnamon sticks*
◇ *3-4 cloves*
◇ *1 tbsp fresh crushed ginger*
◇ *1 tbsp fresh crushed garlic*
◇ *1 tbsp red chilli powder*
◇ *Salt to taste*
◇ *1 small chicken cut in pieces or 300g fish fillets cut in pieces (Bream, Tilapia or Cod) or 300g aubergines*
◇ *¾ cup ghee*

Method

1 Peel the potatoes, cut in half and boil so that they are partially cooked.

2 Drain and then shallow fry them to further cook and brown. Leave aside.

3 Slice the onions thinly and cook in a small amount of oil until browned. Leave aside.

4 Wash the rice and boil with 1 tbsp salt. Drain off the water when half cooked and leave aside.

5 Soak the saffron in 1 tbsp water and leave aside.

6 In a large dish, place yoghurt, cumin seeds, cinnamon sticks, cloves, ginger, garlic and chilli powder and add salt to taste. Mix well. To this add the chicken pieces (braise the chicken pieces in oil with salt, garlic and chilli to taste) or the fillet of fish (marinate the fish in some lemon juice and salt) or the aubergines (cut the aubergines into long pieces and boil with 1 tsp salt).

7 Using a large pot, start the layering process by putting ½ cup ghee or 3 tbsp oil and ½ of the yoghurt mixture (with chicken, fish or aubergine) at the bottom. On top of this, add some fried onions, and potatoes then add some rice to cover. Sprinkle some soaked saffron and repeat this layering process and finish off with a layer of rice on the top.

8 Finally, add the browned onions and sprinkle the saffron mixture over the top.

9 Then add the rest of ghee or 2 tbsp oil and ½ cup water over the top.

10 Cover the lid of the pot with a clean cloth and close the pot tightly. Place this pot over a high heat for a few minutes until it sizzles and then lower the heat to a minimum and cook for about an hour allowing the moisture to cook the rice, potatoes, vegetables, or fish or chicken.

11 Serve this hot with an onion and tomato salad and some plain yoghurt.

The yoghurt can be diluted using 1 cup yoghurt with ¼ cup water. Add salt, diced onions and coriander and serve this with the biryani.

Pilau rice

A SIMPLE VARIANT OF BOILED RICE WITH MORE FLAVOURS AND COLOUR

Preparation time: 5 minutes
Cooking time: 15 minutes
Serves 4

You will need:

◇ *1 cup rice*
◇ *2 tbsp cooking oil*
◇ *A pinch each of cumin seeds and cinnamon*
◇ *1-2 cloves*
◇ *2-3 cardamom pods*
◇ *1 carrot diced*
◇ *½ cup peas*
◇ *1 onion chopped*
◇ *1 tsp salt*
◇ *1-2 cups water*

Method

1 Wash the rice and drain.

2 Heat the oil in a medium pan. Add cumin seeds, cinnamon, cloves and cardamom.

3 When the seeds start to pop add the carrots, peas and onion and stir. Fry for 1-2 minutes.

4 Add the washed rice and salt. Stir and add about a cup of water and lower the heat.

5 Cover the pan with a lid and simmer until the rice is cooked. You may need to add more water if the rice is not cooked.

6 Serve with plain yoghurt.

Khichri

THE ULTIMATE COMFORT FOOD. THE COMBINATION OF RICE AND SPLIT
MOONG DAHL IS AN EXCELLENT REMEDY FOR FLU AND UPSET STOMACHS

Preparation time: 5 minutes
Cooking time: 15-20 minutes
Serves 3-4

You will need:

◇ ½ cup split moong dahl
◇ 1 cup rice

◇ 3 cups water
◇ ½ tsp cumin seeds
◇ ½ tsp tumeric
◇ 1 tsp salt
◇ A pinch of fenugreek seeds (methi)
◇ ¼ tsp fresh chopped garlic
◇ 1 tbsp butter

Method

1 Mix the dahl and rice together and wash well. Boil the water and add the rice/dahl mixture and the rest of the ingredients, except butter.

2 Let it boil and cook.

3 When the rice is cooked, put the lid on and let it steam on low heat. If you prefer the mushy and soft version of khichri, add more water.

4 Just before serving, add the butter and mix. Serve with plain yoghurt.

Khichri can also be cooked with toor dahl. Just replace the split moong dahl with the toor dahl and use the same method of cooking.

Seafood makes you live
10 years more

KEVIN STEELE

SEAFOOD

Steamed fish

TILAPIA IS AN AFRICAN FISH WHICH IS EXTREMELY HEALTHY AND LOW IN FAT

Preparation time: 10 minutes
Cooking time: 25 minutes
Serves 4

You will need:

◇ *300g fish fillets (Tilapia or Sea Bream)*
◇ *A few drops of cooking oil*
◇ *1 tsp salt*
◇ *1 tbsp corn flour*
◇ *1 piece sliced ginger*
◇ *1 tbsp light soy sauce*
◇ *1 tsp chilli powder*
◇ *Spring onion chopped*
◇ *1 chilli thinly sliced*
◇ *1 tbsp oil*
◇ *A few drops of sesame oil*

Method

1 Clean the fish fillets and remove the skin. If you're using frozen fish, take off the skin while it's still frozen (easier to peel).

2 Cut the fish into pieces and rub in the oil and salt. Coat the fish in corn flour.

3 Place the fish in a container which can be used in a steamer.

4 Add ginger, soy sauce and chilli powder to the fish and steam for 10-15 minutes or until cooked.

5 Place the cooked fish in a serving dish. Garnish with chopped spring onions and the sliced chilli.

6 Heat 1 tbsp oil, adding 4-5 drops sesame oil and pour over the steamed fish.

7 Serve hot with boiled rice or rice noodles.

Chef's tip

Tilapia is a delicate, white fish that absorbs flavour very well. It cooks quickly and is easy to prepare. It's best steamed, baked or broiled.

105

Crab
Chinese/Thai style

THERE'S NOTHING QUITE AS FINGER-LICKINGLY SCRUMPTIOUS AS THIS!

Preparation time: 15 minutes
Cooking time: 30 minutes
Serves 6

For the sauce:

◇ 1 tbsp fresh minced ginger
◇ 1 tsp fresh crushed green chillies
◇ 1 tsp red chillies
◇ Salt to taste
◇ 3 tbsp soy sauce
◇ 2 tbsp hoisin sauce
◇ 2 tbsp bean sauce
◇ 2 tbsp oyster sauce
◇ 2 tbsp corn flour
◇ Juice of ½ a lemon

For the crab:

◇ 2 tbsp cooking oil
◇ 1 piece ginger thinly sliced
◇ 5-6 green or red chillies, halved lengthwise
◇ 3kg crab cleaned
◇ ½ bunch green onions cut long to garnish

Method for the sauce

1 Mix all the ingredients and stir well. Keep aside.

Method for the crab

1 Heat the oil and add the sliced ginger and chillies. Stir fry until golden brown and then add the crab.

2 Fry quickly and keep stirring. As the crab starts to turn pink, add the mixed sauce. Add a cup of water and turn down the heat slightly and cover. Allow to simmer for 10 minutes. Keep stirring occasionally, add some more water if required and cook for a further 20 minutes.

3 Let the sauce thicken slightly. Add the green onions and cook for 1-2 minutes. Serve hot.

Curried fish

FISH NORMALLY HAS A BLAND TASTE, SO WHEN COOKED WITH SPICES,
IT LEADS TO AN UNRIVALLED EXOTIC ADVENTURE

Preparation time: 10 minutes
Cooking time: 15 minutes
Serves 4

You will need:

◇ *4 fish fillets (Tilapia, Sea Bream, Hake or Cod)*
◇ *1 tbsp lemon juice*
◇ *Salt to taste*
◇ *1 tbsp cooking oil*
◇ *2 large onions diced*
◇ *1 tbsp fresh crushed garlic*
◇ *1 tbsp red chilli powder*
◇ *1 tbsp tomato purée*
◇ *1 tbsp garam masala*
◇ *Freshly chopped coriander to garnish*

Method

1 Wash and soak the fish fillets using the lemon juice and a pinch of salt.

2 Heat the oil in a pan and braise the diced onions until light brown in colour.

3 Add the garlic, salt, red chilli powder and the tomato purée and cook to a thick sauce.

4 Add the fish to the sauce. Add 2 tbsp water. (If you use frozen fish you do not need to add the water.)

5 Cover the pan with a lid and simmer for 5 minutes or until the fish is cooked.

6 Mix in the garam masala and garnish with chopped coriander.

7 Serve hot.

Masala fish

SPICY AND MOUTH-WATERING, THIS DISH IS QUICK AND EASY TO MAKE

Marination time: 60 minutes
Preparation time: 10 minutes
Cooking time: 20 minutes
Serves 6

You will need:

◇ 300g cleaned sliced and washed fish fillets (Tilapia or Sea Bream)
◇ 1 tbsp salt
◇ ¼ cup lemon juice
◇ 1 tbsp red chilli powder
◇ 1 tbsp fresh crushed ginger
◇ 1 tbsp fresh crushed garlic
◇ 1 tsp gram masala
◇ 1 tsp ground coriander powder
◇ 2 tomatoes grated
◇ 1 tsp tomato purée
◇ 1 tsp fresh crushed green chillies
◇ 1 tsp ground cumin powder
◇ Cooking oil to fry
◇ Freshly chopped coriander to garnish

Method

1 Marinate the fish in salt and 1 tbsp lemon juice and leave in fridge for an hour or so.

2 Drain the excess liquid and shallow fry the fish until cooked. Leave aside.

3 Blend the rest of the ingredients with the remaining lemon juice except the cooking oil.

4 Heat 1 tbsp cooking oil, add the blended mixture and cook for 4-5 minutes until it thickens. Gently pour the mixture over the cooked fish making sure that the fish does not break.

5 Garnish with fresh chopped coriander and serve hot.

Alternatively, you can smear the blended masala on the uncooked marinated fish and bake in an oven at 180°C/350°F/Gas Mark 4 for 20 minutes.

Prawns in black bean sauce

A TANGY BLACK BEAN SAUCE LENDS A RICH FLAVOUR TO SHELLFISH DISHES

Preparation time: 15 minutes
Cooking time: 20 minutes
Serves 4

You will need:

◇ *300g queen prawns*
◇ *1 tsp salt*
◇ *2 tbsp corn flour*
◇ *1 tbsp cooking oil*
◇ *Chilli (optional)*
◇ *2 tbsp black bean sauce*
◇ *1 tsp fresh crushed garlic*

For the broccoli:

◇ *1 cup broccoli florets*
◇ *1 tbsp cooking oil*
◇ *1 tsp fresh crushed garlic*
◇ *A pinch of salt*
◇ *1 tbsp oyster sauce*

Method for the prawns

1 Shell and de-vein the prawns. Remove the heads but keep the tails. Cut open prawns into butterfly shape and stick the tail back.

2 Marinate the prawns in salt, corn flour and 1 tbsp oil and chilli. Leave aside for 10 minutes.

3 Steam the marinated prawns for 4 minutes. Heat the black bean sauce, add the garlic and pour over the prawns and mix. Serve hot.

Method for the broccoli

1 Boil the broccoli florets until the colour changes, drain water and leave aside.

2 Heat the oil in a wok, add garlic, salt and oyster sauce and then the broccoli. Stir once or twice until it is cooked. Decorate the steamed prawns with the seasoned broccoli.

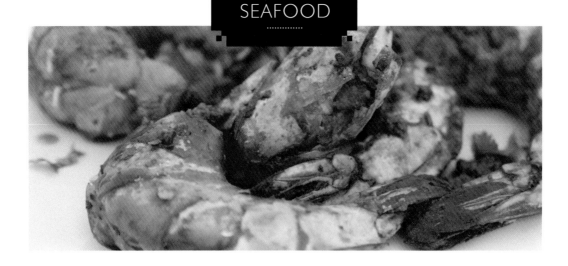

Prawns piri piri

SIMPLE AND QUICK WITH A MIND-BLOWINGLY HOT AND SPICY TASTE

Preparation time: 10 minutes
Cooking time: 15 minutes
Serves 4

You will need:

◇ *300-500g queen or king prawns*
◇ *1 cup lemon juice*
◇ *2 tbsp paprika powder*
◇ *¾ cup butter*
◇ *2 tbsp fresh crushed garlic*
◇ *1 tbsp red chilli powder*
◇ *Salt to taste*
◇ *1 fresh lemon to garnish*

Method

1 Shell and de-vein the prawns. Remove the heads but keep the tails.

2 Cut open prawns into a butterfly shape and stick the tail back.

3 Wash these properly and marinate in 2 tbsp lemon juice with 1 tsp salt and 1 tbsp paprika to give the prawns some colour.

4 To cook the piri piri sauce, melt the butter and add the garlic, chilli powder, remaining paprika, salt and lemon juice. Cook until it is thick and creamy.

5 Add the clean marinated prawns to a hot pan with a tbsp of oil. Braise and cook quickly over high heat. Prawns change colour when cooked to a creamy shade and tails tend to curl up.

6 Place on a platter, garnished with lemon slices. Serve with boiled rice or chips.

The piri piri sauce can be served as a hot dip for the prawns or can be poured over the cooked prawns and mixed.

Coriander fish

A COMBINATION OF HERBS AND CHILLIES MAKES A SUCCULENT FISH DISH

Preparation time: 10 minutes
Cooking time: 20 minutes
Serves 4

You will need:

◇ *300g white fish fillets (Tilapia, Sea Bream, Hake or Cod)*

◇ *½ cup lemon juice*
◇ *2 tbsp olive oil*
◇ *1 medium bunch of coriander washed*
◇ *1 tsp fresh finely chopped garlic*
◇ *1 tsp fresh chopped green chillies*
◇ *Salt and pepper to taste*

Method

1 Wash the fish and soak in 3 tbsp lemon juice.

2 Blend the remaining lemon juice, olive oil, coriander, garlic, green chillies, salt and pepper and pour over washed and soaked fish.

3 Bake in the oven in a covered dish at 160°C/325°F/Gas Mark 4 for 20 minutes.

4 Serve with sautéed potatoes.

Most of the food
allergies die under garlic
and onions

MARTIN H FISCHER

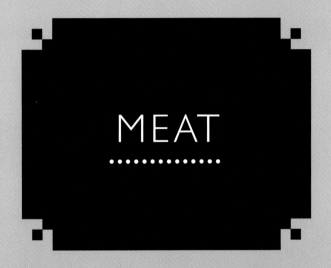

MEAT
·············

Butter chicken

THIS CURRY CREATES AN AWESOME TASTE THAT LINGERS IN THE MOUTH

Preparation time: 10 minutes
Cooking time: 10-15 minutes
Serves 3-4

You will need:

◇ ¼ cup butter
◇ 2 cinnamon sticks
◇ 2 cloves
◇ ½ cup liquidised tomato
◇ 1 tsp garam masala
◇ 1 tsp red chilli powder
◇ 1 tsp crushed garlic
◇ Juice of half a lemon
◇ 1-2 tsp salt
◇ 4 chicken breasts cut in cubes
◇ ¼ cup fresh cream
◇ 1 tbsp ground cashew nuts
◇ Freshly chopped coriander to garnish

Method

1 Melt the butter, then add the cinnamon sticks and the cloves. When they start to sizzle add the tomato, garam masala, chilli powder, garlic, lemon juice, and salt.

2 Marinate the chicken cubes in this and cook on a low heat until tender. Do not overcook, else the chicken will be dry and tough.

3 Add the cream and the ground cashew nuts and simmer for 2-3 minutes.

4 Garnish with coriander and serve hot.

Lamb chops

A GREAT DINNER PARTY FAVOURITE, THESE SUPREMELY TENDER AND SUCCULENT LAMB CHOPS WILL IMPRESS FRIENDS AND FAMILY

Preparation time: 10 minutes
Marination time: 2-3 hours
Cooking time: 30-40 minutes depending on the size of the lamb
Serves 2-3

You will need:

◇ *300g lamb chops*
◇ *1 tbsp fresh crushed garlic*
◇ *1 tbsp fresh crushed ginger*
◇ *1 tbsp tomato purée*
◇ *2 tbsp vinegar or wine or yoghurt*
◇ *2 tbsp cooking oil*
◇ *1 tsp salt*
◇ *1 tbsp fresh crushed green chillies*
◇ *Freshly chopped coriander to garnish*

Method

1 Wash the lamb chops.

2 Make a paste with the rest of ingredients including the oil. Taste for salt and chilli and adjust accordingly.

3 Smear this paste over the lamb chops and leave to marinate for 2-3 hours.

4 Shallow fry in a non-stick frying pan – alternatively, they can be barbecued.

5 Garnish with chopped coriander and serve hot with chips.

Methi chicken with sweetcorn

CHICKEN AND FENUGREEK LEAVES ARE A PERFECT COMBINATION

Preparation time: 15 minutes
Cooking time: 30 minutes
Serves 4-6

You will need:

- ◇ *1 chicken approximately 1kg cut in pieces*
- ◇ *1 cup plain yoghurt*
- ◇ *1 tsp salt*
- ◇ *1 tsp red chilli powder*
- ◇ *2 tsp chopped garlic*
- ◇ *2 tsp fresh chopped ginger*
- ◇ *2 onions sliced*
- ◇ *1 small bunch fenugreek leaves (methi) washed and chopped*
- ◇ *1 tsp turmeric powder*
- ◇ *2 small tomatoes chopped*
- ◇ *1 can sweetcorn*
- ◇ *½ tsp garam masala*
- ◇ *2 tbsp cream*
- ◇ *Freshly chopped coriander to garnish*

Method

1 Marinate the chicken in the yoghurt, salt, red chilli powder, ½ tsp garlic and the ginger for 2 hours.

2 In the meantime, braise the sliced onions, until brown. Add the chopped fenugreek leaves and fry together for 2-3 minutes.

3 Add the rest of the garlic and ginger, a pinch of turmeric powder and mix well. Add the chopped tomatoes and cook for a further 3-5 minutes.

4 Add the marinated chicken. Mix well and allow to cook until the excess water has evaporated. Add the sweetcorn and mix. Taste and adjust salt and chilli. Simmer for 10 minutes.

5 Finally add the garam masala and cream. Cook for a further 5 minutes. Garnish with the coriander and serve with boiled rice or rotis.

Lamb curry

ACCORDING TO MY ENTIRE FAMILY, THIS DISH IS MY SPECIALITY. IT'S FULL OF HOME-COOKED GOODNESS AND NOURISHMENT THROUGHOUT

Preparation time: 15 minutes
Cooking time: Up to 60 minutes
Serves 2-3

You will need:

◇ 500g lamb chops or leg cut in cubes
◇ 2 tbsp cooking oil
◇ 2 cloves
◇ 2 cinnamon sticks
◇ 3 onions finely chopped
◇ 1 tbsp fresh crushed garlic
◇ 1 tbsp fresh crushed ginger
◇ 1 tbsp fresh crushed green chillies
◇ 2 tsp salt
◇ 1 tsp red chilli powder
◇ 3 tomatoes chopped and liquidised
◇ 1 cup water
◇ 1 tsp garam masala
◇ Freshly chopped coriander to garnish

Method

1 Wash the lamb. Heat the oil in a pan, add the cloves, cinnamon sticks and onions. Cook until brown.

2 Add the lamb, garlic, ginger, green chillies, salt and the chilli powder and cook for 5-10 minutes to blend the spices.

3 Add 1 cup water and cover. Allow the lamb to cook. Continue adding water a little at a time until the lamb is tender. It may take up to an hour to tenderise.

4 Add the tomatoes and simmer until the oil particles are visible. Add the garam masala and mix.

5 Taste and adjust for salt and chilli.

6 Garnish with coriander and serve hot with roti, naan, or boiled rice.

Minced meat

KNOWN AS KHEEMA, THIS IS A VERSATILE RECIPE FOR A NUMBER OF DISHES

Preparation time: 10 minutes
Cooking time: Chicken and beef, 20 minutes, lamb 35 minutes
Serves 4

You will need:

◇ *1 large onion diced*
◇ *Cooking oil*
◇ *1 tsp fresh crushed garlic*
◇ *1 tsp fresh crushed ginger*
◇ *300g mince of either chicken, lamb or beef*
◇ *1 tsp salt*
◇ *1 tsp fresh crushed green chillies*
◇ *2 large tomatoes liquidised*
◇ *½ cup water*
◇ *Freshly chopped coriander to garnish*

Method

1 Braise the onion in oil, add the garlic, ginger and cook for 2-3 minutes. Add the meat and stir well.

2 Add the salt and chillies (if green chillies are not available, red chilli powder can be used). Stir and simmer until the meat is cooked.

3 Add the tomatoes and the water. Allow it to come to the boil. Taste and adjust for salt before serving.

4 Garnish with coriander if serving with naan or roti. Garnish with Italian herbs if serving with spaghetti.

Alternatively, you can make meat balls. Season the raw meat with salt, chilli powder and chopped coriander and then make small balls. After braising the onion add the tomatoes, the spices and simmer. Add the meat balls and allow to cook for about 5 minutes. When the meat balls change colour they are cooked. Simmer and garnish before serving.

Pasta with chicken and baked beans

A TASTY, INDIAN-STYLE SPICY PASTA

Preparation time: 10 minutes
Cooking time: 30 minutes
Serves 3-4

You will need:

◇ *250g pasta*
◇ *1 tsp salt*
◇ *300g breast chicken cut into thin strips*
◇ *2 tbsp corn flour*
◇ *Olive oil*
◇ *1 tsp fresh crushed garlic*
◇ *340g can baked beans*
◇ *200g can sweetcorn (optional)*
◇ *1 onion sliced long and thin*
◇ *1 tsp red chilli powder*
◇ *300ml pasta sauce (cooked or ready-made)*
◇ *Grated cheese*

Method

1 Boil the pasta in hot water with the salt and a splash of oil. Keep checking the pasta until it is al dente – this is when there is a little bite left in the centre. Drain and leave aside.

2 Coat the chicken with the corn flour.

3 Heat the oil, add garlic and stir. Add the coated chicken and cook for 5-10 minutes.

4 Mix the baked beans, corn, onion, red chillies and the cooked chicken in a deep baking dish. Add the pasta sauce and finally add the cooked pasta and mix.

5 Sprinkle the grated cheese over the top and bake in an hot oven at 160°C/325°F/Gas Mark 4 for about 20 minutes. Remove from the oven once the cheese has melted.

6 Serve hot with salad.

Chef's tip

Nothing beats this rustic and authentic dish. To cook a great chicken curry, it's best to fry the chicken first.

Chicken curry

THIS RECIPE ORIGINATES IN THE PUNJAB AND IS FULL OF ROBUST FLAVOURS

Preparation time: 10 minutes
Cooking time: 25 minutes
Serves 4-6

You will need:

◇ 1 chicken (approximately 1kg)
◇ 3 tbsp cooking oil
◇ 2 cinnamon sticks
◇ 2 cloves
◇ 2 large onions cubed
◇ 2 tsp salt
◇ 1 tbsp fresh crushed ginger
◇ 1 tbsp fresh crushed garlic
◇ 1 tbsp fresh crushed green chillies
◇ 1 tsp red chilli powder
◇ 1 tsp paprika (optional)
◇ 2 tomatoes liquidised or
400g can peeled tomatoes
◇ 1 tsp tomato purée
◇ 1 tsp garam masala
◇ Freshly chopped coriander to garnish

Method

1 Cut the chicken in pieces and wash thoroughly. These can be washed in a vinegar and water mixture to remove the blood properly.

2 Heat the oil in a medium pan. Add cinnamon sticks, cloves and onions. Fry until brown. Add the washed chicken to this and stir.

3 Add the salt, ginger, garlic and chillies, chilli powder and paprika, if desired. Let it cook until the chicken releases water and changes colour.

4 Add the tomatoes and the tomato purée. Stir and let the chicken cook on a low heat for 15-20 minutes. If you prefer the gravy to be of a thin consistency you can add ½ to 1 cup water.

5 Taste and adjust for salt. Add the garam masala and mix.

6 Garnish with coriander and serve with roti or rice.

Jeera chicken

THE ROASTED CUMIN POWDER
ADDS A SPECIAL ZING

Preparation time: 10 minutes
Cooking time: 20 minutes
Serves 4-6

You will need:

◇ 1 chicken (approximately 1kg)
◇ 3 tbsp cooking oil
◇ 2 cinnamon sticks
◇ 2 cloves
◇ 1 tsp cumin seeds
◇ 2 large onions sliced
◇ 2 tsp salt
◇ 1 tbsp fresh crushed ginger
◇ 1 tbsp fresh crushed garlic
◇ 1 tbsp fresh crushed green chillies
◇ 2 tsp garam masala
◇ 2 tsp coriander powder
◇ 3 tsp roasted cumin powder
◇ Freshly chopped coriander to garnish

Method

1 Cut the chicken in pieces and thoroughly wash in a vinegar and water mixture to remove the blood properly.

2 Heat the oil in a medium pan. Add cinnamon sticks, cloves, cumin seeds and onions. Fry until brown. Add the washed chicken to this and stir.

3 Add the salt, ginger, garlic and chillies, garam masala, coriander powder and cumin powder and let it cook until the chicken releases water and changes colour.

4 Stir and let the chicken cook on a low heat for 10-15 minutes.

5 Taste and adjust for salt.

6 Garnish with coriander and serve.

Sweet and sour chicken

THE CONTRASTING TASTES OF SWEET
AND SOUR SENDS YOUR TASTEBUDS
INTO AN OUTRIGHT FRENZY

Preparation time:
10 minutes
Cooking time:
15 minutes
Serves 4

You will need:

◇ 3 chicken breasts
◇ 3 tbsp corn flour
◇ 2 tbsp cooking oil
◇ 1 tsp fresh garlic
◇ 2 whole tomatoes frozen
◇ ½ cup sugar
◇ 1 tsp salt
◇ 6 tbsp brown vinegar
◇ 2 tbsp tomato sauce
◇ 1 can sliced pineapple
◇ 1 green pepper sliced
◇ 1 red pepper sliced
◇ 1 tsp paprika
◇ 1½ cups water

Method

1 Slice the chicken breasts into thin strips and coat with 2 tbsp corn flour. Heat oil in a pan and add garlic and shallow fry the chicken strips for 2-3 minutes. Put to one side.

2 Remove the skin from the tomatoes by dipping them in hot water and slice them. Remove seeds.

3 To prepare the sauce, heat 1 tbsp oil and add the skinned tomatoes. Add sugar, salt, vinegar and tomato sauce. Cover pan and allow to simmer.

4 Add 1 cup water and mix. When mixed add the sliced pineapple, the peppers and the paprika.

5 Dissolve 1 tbsp corn flour in ½ cup water and add this slowly to the sauce. This will thicken the sauce. Allow to simmer for 5 minutes.

6 Taste and adjust for sourness by adding more vinegar. If it's not sour enough, add sugar to sweeten.

7 Add the chicken to the sauce and simmer for 2-3 minutes. Serve with rice.

Marinated spare ribs

SERVE THESE JUICY, TENDER RIBS WITH HOT CHIPS AND A FRESH SALAD

Preparation time: 10 minutes
Marination time: 2-3 hours
Cooking time: 30 minutes
Serves 4

You will need:

◇ *1 rack of pork ribs (1.5kg)*
◇ *2 tsp mixed herbs*
◇ *1 tsp salt*
◇ *4 tbsp apricot jam*
◇ *4 tbsp vinegar*
◇ *2 tbsp tomato sauce*
◇ *2-3 tbsp worcester sauce*

Method

1 Remove the flap and extra fat from the ribs and score all over with a sharp knife.

2 Boil the spare ribs in water, herbs and salt until cooked.

3 Prepare the sauce by mixing the jam, vinegar, tomato sauce and the worcester sauce.

4 Baste the prepared sauce over the ribs and leave for at least 2 hours.

5 Cook in a preheated oven at 160°C/325°F/Gas Mark 3 for about 30 minutes. You may have to add a little water if the sauce evaporates.

6 Baste the ribs with the sauce during cooking and turn over several times.

7 Serve with hot chips and salad.

Lasagne

A HEARTY MEAL THAT KEEPS BOTH VEGETARIANS AND MEAT EATERS HAPPY

Preparation time:
20 minutes
Cooking time:
50 minutes
Serves 4-6

You will need:

◇ 1 large onion diced
◇ Cooking or olive oil
◇ 1 tsp fresh crushed garlic
◇ 1 tsp fresh crushed ginger
◇ 300g mince of either chicken, lamb or beef
◇ 1 tsp salt
◇ 1 tsp fresh crushed green chillies
◇ 2 large tomatoes liquidised
◇ ½ cup water
◇ 250g lasagne pasta (the type that requires no pre-cooking)
◇ 250ml cheese sauce (150g cream or cottage cheese, 50ml milk, 50ml water, salt and pepper blended together)
◇ 1 cup grated mozzarella

Method

1 Braise the onion in some oil. Add the garlic and ginger and cook for 2-3 minutes. Add the minced meat and stir well. Add the salt and chillies and stir. Simmer until the meat is cooked.

2 Add the tomatoes and ½ cup water and bring to the boil. Add more water to give it a runny consistency. (The no pre-cooking lasagne requires a lot of fluid, else the lasagne will be raw and dry.)

3 Layer the lasagne in a large oven-proof dish by placing the lasagne at the bottom of the dish, overlapping if necessary. Drizzle 2 tbsp cheese sauce to cover the lasagne.

4 Spread about 2-3 tbsp cooked meat on top of the lasagne and cheese sauce. Sprinkle over grated mozzarella and add 2-3 tbsp water. Repeat the layering process finishing with a lasagna layer at the top. Make sure there's plenty of fluid for cooking. Sprinkle over the remaining cheese.

5 Cover the dish with foil or a lid and bake in a preheated oven at 160°C/325°F/Gas Mark 3 for 20-30 minutes. Remove foil and serve hot with a crispy salad.

For a vegetarian alternative, substitute the meat with diced aubergine or spinach.

Shepherd's pie

A CLASSIC AND TRADITIONAL BRITISH DISH FUSED WITH INDIAN SPICES

Preparation time: 10 minutes
Cooking time: 20 minutes
Serves 4

You will need:

◇ *1 large onion diced*
◇ *Cooking oil*
◇ *1 tsp fresh crushed garlic*
◇ *1 tsp fresh crushed ginger*
◇ *300g mince of either chicken, lamb or beef*
◇ *1 tsp salt*
◇ *1 tsp fresh crushed green chillies*
◇ *2 large tomatoes liquidised*
◇ *½ cup water*
◇ *3 large potatoes boiled and mashed*
◇ *Salt to taste*
◇ *1 tbsp butter*

Method

1 Braise the onion in some oil and add the garlic and ginger and cook for 2-3 minutes. Add the minced meat and stir well.

2 Add the salt and chillies, stir and simmer until the meat is cooked.

3 Add the tomatoes and roughly ½ cup water and bring to the boil. Leave aside.

4 Mix the mashed potatoes with the salt and butter.

5 Place the cooked meat at the bottom of an oven-proof dish. Cover this with the mashed potatoes. Using a fork, rake the potato mash to give it a design.

6 Bake at 160°C/325°F/Gas Mark 3 for 10 minutes or until golden brown.

7 Serve hot with gravy.

For a vegetarian alternative, omit the minced meat and use mixed vegetables.

I want to have a good
body, but not as much
as I want dessert

JASON LOVE

DESSERTS

· · · · · · · · · · · · ·

Apple pie

SERVED STEAMING HOT, THIS IS THE PERFECT PICK-ME-UP ON A COLD NIGHT

Preparation time: 15 minutes
Cooking time: 45 minutes
Serves 8

You will need:

◇ 8 apples small
◇ ½ cup water
◇ ¼ cup sugar
◇ 2 slices of lemon
◇ 1 tsp cinnamon powder

For the pastry:

◇ 2 cups cake flour
◇ 1 tsp baking powder
◇ 1 cup sugar
◇ 115g + 50g margarine
◇ 2 egg yolks
◇ 1 egg whole
◇ 1 tbsp sugar
◇ A sprinkle of chopped almonds or pecan nuts

Method

1 Peel and slice the apples. Boil them in water with the sugar and lemon slices. Cook for 10 minutes.

2 Add the cinnamon and cook for a further 2 minutes. Alternatively, use tinned apple or any other tinned fruit filling. Just add the cinnamon to your chosen fruit and use as a filling.

3 To make the pastry, combine all the ingredients except margarine, sugar and nuts, and knead gently. When the dough is kneaded to a soft consistency, put 1 cup pastry aside in the fridge to harden. Now, using your hands, layer the rest of it in a medium pie dish. The dough will be fairly soft so gently press it down onto the dish. Spread the apple filling on the pastry. Add the 50g margarine on top of the filling. Grate the pastry, which you have put aside in the fridge, over the apple filling.

4 Sprinkle over the sugar and nuts and bake for 45 minutes at 190°C/375°F/Gas Mark 5.

5 Serve hot with custard or cream.

Crunchies

THE BEAUTY OF THIS RECIPE IS THAT IT TAKES MINUTES TO MAKE – WHICH
IS IDEAL BECAUSE IT IS IMPOSSBLE TO EAT JUST ONE!

Preparation time: 10 minutes
Cooking time: 15-20 minutes
Serves 8

You will need:

◇ *200g margarine*
◇ *3 tbsp golden syrup*
◇ *2 cups oats*
◇ *1 cup desiccated coconut*
◇ *1 cup cake flour*
◇ *1 cup sugar*
◇ *1 tbsp bicarbonate of soda*
◇ *A pinch of salt*

Method

1 Combine the margarine with the syrup and gently heat until melted.

2 Sift the remaining dry ingredients together and pour over the margarine mixture and mix well.

3 Press out onto a baking tray (approx 23cm square) and bake at 190°C/375°F/Gas Mark 5 for 15-20 minutes until golden brown.

4 Mark into squares while still hot, then slice once cooled. Store in an airtight container.

Banana muffins

A HEALTHY AFTERNOON SNACK THAT GOES GREAT WITH A CUP OF TEA

Preparation time: 20 minutes
Cooking time: 20-25 minutes
(10-15 minutes for mini muffins)
Makes 4-5 large muffins or 12 mini muffins

◇ *1 tbsp water*
◇ *1 tsp vanilla essence*
◇ *1 tsp nutmeg powder*
◇ *1 cup cake flour*
◇ *½ tsp salt*

You will need:

◇ *¾ cup sugar*
◇ *115g margarine*
◇ *1 cup mashed ripe banana*
◇ *1 tsp bicarbonate of soda*

For the topping:

◇ *3 tsp dark brown sugar*
◇ *2 tsp cinnamon powder*
◇ *½ cup chopped pecan nuts*

Method

1 Cream together the sugar and margarine. Add the mashed bananas and mix.

2 Dissolve the bicarbonate of soda in the water and add to the banana mixture.
Add the vanilla essence.

3 Mix the nutmeg with the flour and combine well with the banana mixture.

4 Using a muffin tray add about 1 tbsp of mixture for each muffin. (For the mini muffins
you can use a mini muffin tray and less mixture.)

5 Mix the topping ingredients and sprinkle a little over each muffin.

6 Bake in a preheated oven at 180°C/350°F/Gas Mark 4 until golden brown.

Cheese scones

THIS QUICK AND TASTY SNACK CAN BE ENJOYED ON ITS OWN

Preparation time: 5 minutes
Cooking time: 15 minutes
Serves 6

You will need:

◇ 4 tbsp cake flour
◇ ½ tsp baking powder
◇ ¼ tsp salt
◇ 1 tbsp cooking oil
◇ 1 tbsp grated cheese heaped
◇ 1 whole egg or 2 tbsp milk to bind

Method

1 Sieve all dry ingredients together. Rub the oil into the flour, lifting the flour, airing it, until everything is mixed in.

2 Add cheese and mix lightly.

3 Make a well in the centre and add either the egg or milk and bind lightly.

4 Lift large lumps of mixture and place onto an oiled tray. No rolling or cutting is required.

5 Bake at 220°C/425°F/Gas Mark 7 for 15 minutes or until golden brown.

Carrot cake with icing

A WHOLESOME AND FILLING TREAT

Preparation time: 10 minutes
Cooking time: 55 minutes
Serves 6-8

◇ 1 tbsp cinnamon
◇ 1 tbsp bicarbonate of soda
◇ 1 tsp nutmeg
◇ A pinch of salt

You will need:

◇ 750g grated carrots
◇ 3 eggs beaten
◇ 100g pecans or walnuts
◇ 250ml cooking oil
◇ 300g sugar
◇ 180g cake flour

For the icing:

◇ 50g cottage cheese or cream cheese
◇ 1 tbsp lemon juice
◇ Icing sugar to decorate

Method

1 Mix together carrots, beaten eggs, nuts, oil and sugar in a large bowl.

2 Sift the rest of the ingredients and mix well.

3 Pour in a greased cake tin and bake in a preheated oven at 180°C/350°F/Gas Mark 4 for around 1 hour.

4 To prepare the icing, mix all icing ingredients together. The consistency should be slightly runny.

5 Pour this onto the cake and decorate with some pecan nuts.

Cheese icing can be omitted and the cake can be decorated simply by sprinkling icing sugar and pecan nuts over the top.

Jalebi

THESE SWEET BITES ARE BEST SERVED ON THE SAME DAY THEY'RE MADE

Preparation time: 15 minutes
Cooking time: 40 minutes
Serves 8-10

You will need:

◇ *3 cups sugar*
◇ *1½ cups water*
◇ *A pinch of ground cardamom*
◇ *1 tbsp lemon juice*

◇ *A pinch of yellow food colouring*

For the jalebi:

◇ *1 cup of cake flour*
◇ *1 tbsp baking powder*
◇ *2 tbsp ghee*
◇ *Cooking oil to fry*
◇ *Greaseproof paper*

Method

1 Prepare the syrup, add the sugar to the water and boil on a slow heat for 10-15 minutes until just sticky. To check the consistency, hold up the spoon and if a drop falls off from it, it is ready.

2 Add the cardamom powder, yellow food colouring and the lemon juice and keep the syrup aside ready for soaking the jalebi.

3 Mix the flour, baking powder and ghee in a blender to get a runny consistency, with no lumps. Pour this in a plastic, squeezy bottle with a small hole on the cap (see above).

4 Heat the oil in a shallow frying pan. The temperature of the oil is critical so make it very hot first then let it cool to a medium heat before frying.

5 Using the plastic bottle, squeeze out circles in a spiral form from the inside out. The jalebi should not float onto the oil too fast nor stay at the bottom for too long. Fry and turn so that both sides are cooked. Drain the oil and soak in the ready syrup.

6 Soak in the syrup for 1-2 minutes and drain on a rack (e.g. a wired oven shelf, placed on a plate to allow the excess syrup to drain off). When cool, store in a container in layers of jalebi and greaseproof paper.

Chef's tip

These pancakes are delicious with maple syrup. Just perfect for an everyday breakfast or brunch.

Pancake dessert

NO TIME FOR LONG-WINDED OR COMPLICATED DESSERTS? THIS IS YOUR BEST BET. IT'S QUICK YET LOOKS AND TASTES DIVINE. TUCK IN

Preparation time: 5 minutes
Cooking time: 15 minutes
Serves 4-6

You will need:

◇ ½ cup cake flour
◇ ½ cup milk
◇ 1 large egg
◇ ½ tsp baking powder
◇ A pinch of salt
◇ 1 tbsp cooking oil
◇ Ice-cream (scoop for each pancake)
◇ A drizzle of maple syrup
◇ A handful of roasted nuts to decorate

Method

1 Blend the flour, milk, egg, baking powder and salt to make the pancake batter.

2 Heat a non-stick pan or a slightly oiled pan on medium heat. Pour 2 tbsp of the pancake batter and add about 1 tsp oil around the perimeter of the pancake.

3 Turn the pancake to cook the other side. Add a little more oil turning again until the pancake is cooked to a golden brown colour.

4 Just before serving, place a scoop of ice cream on one side of the pancake and roll so that the ice cream is sandwiched.

5 Drizzle over some maple syrup and sprinkle nuts to decorate. Serve

Chocolate cake with frosting

IDEAL ON A HOT DAY WITH A COLD GLASS OF MILK FOR A CALCIUM BOOST

Preparation time: 15 minutes
Cooking time: 35 minutes
Serves 6-8

You will need:

◇ 2 cups icing sugar
◇ 2 cups cake or self raising flour
◇ ¾ cup cocoa powder
◇ 1½ tsp baking powder
◇ 1½ tsp bicarbonate of soda
◇ 1 tsp salt
◇ 2 eggs
◇ ½ cup cooking oil
◇ 2 tsp vanilla essence
◇ 1 cup milk
◇ 1 cup boiling hot water

For the frosting:

◇ ½ cup butter
◇ ¾ cup cocoa powder
◇ 3 cups icing sugar
◇ ¼ cup milk
◇ 1 tsp vanilla essence

Method for the cake

1 Sift all the dry ingredients in a bowl.

2 In a second bowl, beat the eggs with the oil, vanilla and milk and pour in the dry mixture.

3 Mix together well. Add the cup of boiling water and mix. The consistency of batter should be runny.

4 Pour it into a non-stick prepared 23cm cake tin and bake at 180°C/350°F/Gas Mark 4 for 30-35 minutes.

Method for the frosting

1 To make the frosting, melt the butter in the microwave and beat in the remaining ingredients to create the consistence of a sauce.

2 Once ready, pour the frosting over the cake to decorate.

3 Leave in the fridge before serving.

4 The frosting might be too much for the cake but can be left in fridge to be used again.

Peda

IT IS AN INDIAN TRADITION TO GIVE OUT PEDAS TO FAMILIES AND FRIENDS
TO MARK THE HAPPY OCCASION WHEN A BABY BOY IS BORN

Preparation time: 10 minutes
Cooking time: 25 minutes
Serves 8-15

You will need:

◇ *3 cups full cream powdered milk*

◇ *2 cups icing sugar*
◇ *½ tsp ground cardamom*
◇ *2 tbsp sweetened condensed milk*
◇ *1 tbsp ghee melted*
◇ *½ tsp rose essence*
◇ *½ cup cream*
◇ *Almond flakes to decorate*

Method

1 Sift together all the dry ingredients into a large mixing bowl.

2 Combine the remaining ingredients and pour over the dry mixture.

3 Using a wooden spoon, mix together contents until a smooth dough is formed.

4 Break off small pieces, rub and make into round shapes with greased palms or you can use a peda mould (as shown above).

5 Take a few almond flakes and press them down on each peda.

6 Place on a tray to dry.

7 Store in an airtight container.

Gulab jamun

THESE LITTLE BALLS OF FUN GIVE YOU THAT IRRESISTIBLE MELT IN YOUR MOUTH SENSATION AND LEAVE YOU FEELING COSY AND WARM INSIDE

Preparation time: 15 minutes
Cooking time: 40 minutes
Serves 8

For the syrup:

◇ 2½ cups sugar
◇ 1 cup water
◇ 2 drops rose water

For the balls:

◇ 1 cup powdered milk
◇ 2 tbsp cake flour
◇ 2 tbsp ghee
◇ 1 tsp baking powder
◇ ¼ cup cold milk
◇ Cooking oil to fry

Method

1 Prepare the syrup by simply mixing the sugar and water. Stir until dissolved. Boil for about 15 minutes and take off the heat.

2 Cool to room temperature and add the drops of rose water, to flavour.

3 To make the balls, first mix together the powdered milk, flour, ghee and baking powder. The mixture should feel sticky in your fist. Knead the mixture with a small amount of cold milk until the dough softens. Knead for a further 2 minutes.

4 Pinch a small amount of the dough and roll into small balls and smooth out by rolling between your palms.

5 Heat the oil and test the temperature by dropping a pea-sized bit of dough into the pan. It should float gently to the top and start rolling over. Reduce the heat if it turns brown straightaway.

6 Fry on medium to low heat until golden brown. Drain on a paper towel. Then add to the syrup and let them soak for 1-2 hours to absorb the syrup. Serve hot or cold or with ice cream.

Chocolate fridge cake

THIS CHOCOLATE CAKE IS STUNNING. EASY, SCRUMPTIOUS AND NO BAKING REQUIRED – IT WILL KEEP ALMOST FOREVER IN THE FRIDGE

Preparation time: 15-20 minutes
Serves 4-6

You will need:

◇ Greaseproof paper
◇ 2 eggs
◇ 2 tbsp sugar
◇ 225g margarine melted
◇ 225g plain chocolate melted over hot water
◇ 1½ packet marie biscuits crushed
◇ ½ cup chopped nuts
◇ 10 glace cherries chopped
◇ 2 drops of vanilla essence (or almond essence or 1 tsp coffee powder)

Method

1 Line a loaf tin with greaseproof paper. If you are using a non-stick tin then there's no need for lining.

2 Beat the eggs thoroughly and add sugar and melted margarine pouring slowly while hot.

3 Add melted chocolate a small amount at a time, beating it with a wooden spoon.

4 Add the biscuits, nuts, cherries and the essence. Fold until biscuits are well coated with chocolate.

5 Put in the loaf tin and flatten the surface. Place in the fridge to chill until firm.

6 Cut into slices and serve. Store in the fridge.

Nan khatai

A DELICIOUS TEA-TIME BITE FOR ALL

Preparation time: 15 minutes
Cooking time: 10 minutes
Serves 6-8

You will need:

◇ 1 cup ghee
◇ 1 cup caster sugar
◇ 1½ cup cake flour
◇ ½ cup gram flour
◇ 1 tsp baking powder
◇ ½ tsp bicarbonate of soda
◇ 1 tsp ground cardamom
◇ ½ tsp nutmeg
◇ ½ cup semolina

Method

1 Whip together the ghee and the castor sugar. Sieve the rest of the ingredients twice over and add to the ghee and castor sugar mixture.

2 Mix well and knead to a moist dough.

3 Make small balls. Lightly press each ball between your palms. Using a matchstick draw a cross on the top of each ball. Alternatively you can press an almond on top of each ball.

4 Place these balls 1 in apart on a baking tray and bake at 180°C/380°F/Gas Mark 4 for 10 minutes.

5 Cool and store in airtight container.

Dry gulab jamun with coconut

WHEN YOU'RE CRAVING SOMETHING SWEET, HAVE A COUPLE OF THESE!

Preparation time: 15 minutes
Cooking time: 60 minutes
Serves 10-12

For the syrup:

◊ 2½ cups water
◊ 2½ cups sugar
◊ 1 tsp lemon juice

For the gulab jamun:

◊ 2½ cups self raising flour
◊ 1 cup semolina
◊ ½ cup ghee
◊ ½ cup plain yoghurt
◊ 3 tbsp baking powder
◊ 1 can sweetened condensed milk
◊ 1 tsp ground cardamom seeds (optional)
◊ 1 tsp powdered nutmeg (optional)
◊ Cooking oil to fry
◊ 1 cup desiccated coconut

Method for the syrup

1 Mix and boil the water and sugar for 10 minutes.

2 Cool to room temperature and the add the lemon juice.

Method for the gulab jamun

1 Combine all the ingredients except the coconut and knead well for 5-10 minutes to a soft dough.

2 Pinch small portions of the dough and roll into oval or long balls. Fry a few at a time on a medium heat until dark brown in colour.

3 Soak in the syrup for 1-2 minutes and drain on a rack (e.g. a wired rack from the oven placed on a plate to allow excess syrup to drain off).

4 Now, roll the balls in the coconut, and lay them in a single layer until cool.

5 Store in an airtight container.

Eggless cake

SOFT, TASTY AND INNOVATIVE, THIS IS IDEAL FOR VEGETARIANS AND VEGANS

Preparation time: 10 minutes
Cooking time: 35 minutes
Serves 6-8

You will need

◇ Greaseproof paper
◇ 2½ cups cake flour
◇ 2 tsp baking powder
◇ 1 tsp bicarbonate of soda
◇ ¼ tbsp salt
◇ 2 tsp sugar
◇ 397ml can condensed milk
◇ 1 cup water (or freshly squeezed fruit juice such as orange, pineapple, passion fruit)
◇ 2 tbsp vinegar
◇ 2 tbsp vanilla essence
◇ ½ cup melted butter

Method

1 Preheat the oven at 180°C/350°F/Gas Mark 4 for 15 minutes.

2 Lightly grease a 23cm cake tin and line with greaseproof paper.

3 In a large bowl, sift together the flour, baking powder, bicarbonate soda and salt. Add sugar to this mixture.

4 Make a well in the middle of the dry ingredients and stir in the wet ingredients one at a time. Stir the mixture together using a whisk. If using fresh orange juice, you can also add the grind of an orange peel.

5 Pour it into the prepared cake tin, tap the tin to even it out and to remove any air bubbles.

6 Bake for 25-35 minutes.

7 Allow to cool and remove cake from tin after 15-20 minutes. Slice and serve when completely cool.

Kulfi

ONE OF THE MOST POPULAR INDIAN RESTAURANT DESSERTS WHICH CAN BE DESCRIBED AS THE INDIAN VERSION OF ITALIAN GELATO!

Preparation time: 30 minutes
Freezing time: 2 hours
Serves 6-8

For mango kulfi:

◇ 2 x 380g frozen cans evaporated milk
◇ 250ml packet fresh cream
◇ ¾ x 397ml can condensed milk
◇ 2 cups mango pulp

For pistachio kulfi:

◇ 2 x 380g frozen cans evaporated milk
◇ 250ml packet fresh cream
◇ ¾ x 397ml can condensed milk
◇ 2 tbsp pistachio nuts (diced or powdered)
◇ 3 tbsp chopped almonds

Method

1 Freeze the evaporated milk cans overnight.

2 Beat the fresh cream to a thick consistency using an electric beater. Add condensed milk followed by the frozen evaporated milk. Beat again to mix well.

3 For the mango kulfi: add the mango pulp and mix well.

4 For pistachio kulfi: add the pistachio nuts and the chopped almonds and mix well.

5 Pour into individual kulfi moulds or an ice cream container and freeze until ready to serve.

Shrikhand

A FAVOURITE DESSERT AT GUJARATI WEDDINGS AND SPECIAL EVENTS

Preparation time: Drain overnight
Cooking time: 30 minutes
Serves 6

You will need:

◇ *2 x 500ml plain yoghurt*
◇ *1 cup cream cheese*
◇ *1 cup cottage cheese*
◇ *1¼ cups caster sugar*
◇ *½ tsp ground cardamom*
◇ *Ground pistachio nuts and almonds to decorate*
◇ *A pinch of dry saffron*

Method

1 Drain the yoghurt in a colander over a muslin cloth and keep in a cool place, preferably overnight so the yoghurt hardens.

2 The following day, mix both the cheeses with the yoghurt and add the sugar.

3 Sieve this mixture through a muslin cloth. (To do this, tie the muslin cloth onto a deep steel dish and then sieve through with either a spoon or hand.) If the mixture is very stiff then add a little cream or milk. Alternatively, instead of sieving the mixture, it can be blended together but you may find you need to add more cream to get the correct consistency, which is that of custard.

4 Add the cardamom and mix.

5 Serve in a glass dish and decorate with the pistachio nuts and almonds and a pinch of saffron.

6 Keep it in the fridge before serving

Kheer

AN AUSPICIOUS PUDDING IN INDIA THAT IS ALSO SERVED IN GURDWARAS

Preparation time: 10 minutes
Cooking time: 20 minutes
Serves 6

You will need:

◇ *¼ cup rice*
◇ *500ml milk*
◇ *250ml cream*
◇ *¼ cup sugar*
◇ *3 tbsp ground almonds*
◇ *Blanched almonds to decorate*
◇ *1 tsp ground cardamom*

Method

1 Boil the rice in about ½ cup of water until cooked.

2 Boil the milk separately until it thickens and reduces. Add the boiled rice and continue to boil until the rice swells.

3 Add the cream. Stir well and add the sugar. Add the ground almonds, stirring all the time.

4 When the mixture thickens remove from the heat.

5 Cut the blanched almonds (boiled and skinned almonds) into thirds and add to the rice pudding. Add the cardamom and mix.

6 Cool in the fridge before serving.

Pineapple mousse

A MOUTHFUL OF THIS DESSERT WILL TAKE YOU TO AN EXOTIC DESTINATION

Preparation time: 10 minutes
Cooking time: 10 minutes
excluding setting time
Serves 6

You will need:

◇ *80g packet pineapple jelly*
◇ *Boiling water*
◇ *250ml packet fresh cream*
◇ *385g can pineapple chunks in syrup*

Method

1 Dissolve the contents of the jelly as per packet instructions, but instead of using boiling water only, use a mixture of half water and half syrup from the canned pineapple. Stir until dissolved.

2 Place in a fridge until half set, should not be firm.

3 When the jelly is half set, liquidise all of it with the drained pineapple chunks and the packet of fresh cream.

4 Pour into mousse cups or in a large dish and place in the fridge to set.

5 When firm, decorate with fresh pineapple or desiccated coconut and serve.

Chef's tip

Adding nuts while the vermicelli is cooking makes them soft and delicious.

Vermicelli kheer

A GREAT DESSERT FOR GUESTS WHEN CELEBRATING A HAPPY OCCASION

Preparation time: 10 minutes
Cooking time: 20 minutes
Serves 6

You will need:

◇ *1 cup vermicelli*
◇ *1 tbsp ghee*
◇ *1-2 cups milk*
◇ *½ cup sugar*
◇ *1 cup fresh cream*
◇ *2 tbsp chopped almonds*

Method

1 Fry the vermicelli in the ghee on a low heat until it turns light brown in colour.

2 Add milk to this and stir. Bring to the boil and add the sugar.

3 Simmer for 2-3 minutes to allow the milk to thicken and the vermicelli to swell up. Add the cream, stirring all the time. As the mixture thickens add the almonds.

4 Remove from the heat, taste and adjust the sweetness as desired.

5 This can be served hot or cold.

Semolina pudding

THIS IS GIVEN AS AN OFFERING IN TEMPLES AND GURDWARAS AND ALSO AT HAVANS

Preparation time:
10 minutes
Cooking time:
15 minutes
Serves 4

You will need:

◇ 1 cup milk
◇ *1½ cups water*
◇ *¾ cup sugar*
◇ *1 cup ghee*
◇ *1 cup semolina*
◇ *Chopped almonds and pistachio nuts to decorate*
◇ *Crushed cardamom seeds to decorate*

Method

1 Using a medium pan, boil the milk and the water. Add sugar and allow to dissolve.

2 Melt the ghee in a separate pot on a medium heat, add semolina and stir until the mixture turns an almond colour.

3 Add the milk and water mixture to the semolina, a small amount at a time, stirring continuously till the mixture is absorbed and thickened.

4 Remove the pan from the heat, but carry on stirring until the semolina comes off the sides and the ghee is floating.

5 Put it back on a low heat and continue stirring.

6 Taste for sugar, and adjust if necessary. Finally add chopped nuts and crushed cardamom seeds.

7 Remove from the heat and serve.

Alternatively, omit the milk and use 2½ cups of water only. You can also substitute semolina with whole wheat flour.

Cappuccino mousse

AS THEY SAY SOME THINGS ARE BETTER RICH, WHAT MORE THAN COMBINATION OF CHOCOLATE AND COFFEE!

Preparation time: 5 minutes
Cooking time: 15minutes
excluding setting time
Serves 6

You will need:

◇ *397ml can sweetened condensed milk*
◇ *⅓ cup cocoa powder*
◇ *3 tbsp butter*
◇ *2 tbsp instant coffee*
◇ *2 tbsp hot water*
◇ *2 cups double cream chilled*

Method

1 Combine condensed milk, cocoa, butter, coffee (dissolved in hot water) in a medium pan.

2 Cook over a low heat, stirring constantly until the butter completely melts and the mixture has a smooth texture.

3 Whip the double cream in a large bowl until it stiffens.

4 Gradually fold the chocolate mixture into the whipped cream.

5 Spoon into dessert dishes and refrigerate for around 2 hours until set.

6 To decorate the mousse add a dollop of fresh cream before serving.

Ghooghra

YOU KNOW IT IS TIME TO CELEBRATE WHEN YOU GET TO EAT GHOOGHRA!

Preparation time:
30 minutes
Cooking time: 60 minutes
Serves: 20

For the filling:

◇ *½ cup ghee*

◇ *225g semolina*
◇ *110g desiccated coconut*
◇ *1 cup ground almonds and pistachio mixture*
◇ *500g sugar*
◇ *½ cup gram flour*
◇ *1 tsp ground cloves*
◇ *½ tbsp ground cardamom seeds*

For the pastry:

◇ *3-4 tbsp ghee*
◇ *3 cups cake flour*
◇ *½-1 cup warm milk*
◇ *Cooking oil to fry*

Method

1 Warm the ghee (leaving about 2 tbsp from the ½ cup for roasting the gram flour) in a medium pan.

2 Add the semolina and stir until the mixture turns beige. Make sure it does not turn brown. (The tip is to stir just until you smell the flavour being dispersed.)

3 Take the pan off the heat and add the coconut, nuts and sugar and stir well. Keep aside.

4 In a separate pan, roast the gram flour in 2 tbsp ghee. Stir until the flavour disperses. It should be slightly brown in colour. Remove from the heat.

5 Now add this to the semolina mixture along with cloves and ground cardamom seeds.

6 Allow to cool in a large dish but do not cover the dish. When cold, massage the mixture between your hands. Leave aside until ready to fill the pastry. (This mixture can be cooked in advance and left in the fridge to use as a filling at a later stage.)

7 Mix in the ghee with flour. When you can make a fist of this mixture then the amount of ghee is right. Add a small amount of warm milk at a time and knead to a soft dough. Cover with a damp cloth.

8 Divide the dough into small balls and roll out each ball to a circle of about 5cm in diameter.

9 Place 1 tsp of filling in the middle of the pastry circle and pinch the ends so that the filling does not spill when the ghoogras are fried. (This can be difficult so you could use a small pie cutter for the same effect.)

10 When filled, fry the Ghoogras on a slow heat till slightly brown. Cool and store in an airtight container.

IKEBANA

The earth laughs in flowers

RALPH WALDO EMERSON

INTRODUCTION

I moved to Harare, Zimbabwe in 1991. It was fashionable in those days for young ladies to learn the art of flower arranging and my mother-in-law's wish was for me to do so, too. One of the reasons our spacious garden is so picturesque was because my mother-in-law was a keen gardener. With three young kids in tow, and a life-changing move with my husband to a new country, combined with working as a pharmacist full-time, I barely had any spare free time. However, I would attend flower exhibitions with my mother-in-law and I soon found that I quite enjoyed them. Almost ten years later, in 2002, I attended my first Ikebana exhibition and absolutely loved it. And with my kids more grown-up by this time, I decided to find out exactly what Ikebana is all about.

Ikebana. Even its name is flower like. It's described as the Japanese art of flower arrangement – but it is so much more than simply putting flowers in a container. Ikebana is a disciplined art form in which nature and humanity are brought together. Like most things Japanese, it's an employment of minimalism. Over the seven centuries of its evolution, Ikebana has developed many different styles of arrangement and hence there are many different schools. I was fortunate enough to learn from the teachings of Sogetsu. Sogetsu School of Ikebana was founded by Sofu Teshigahara in 1927. The well-known sculptor and Ikebana master gave new impetus to modern trends, so that modern and abstract arrangements are made. His motto was 'Ikebana anywhere, anytime with any material'.

I started my lessons with Lyn Pozzo who, at the time, was president of the Ikebana chapter of Harare. The curriculum of Sogetsu consists of four textbooks with 20 lessons each. Working with Lyn, who was very patient with me, I completed the first textbook. Unfortunately soon after this, she stopped teaching. And due to economics and politics, we lost our Harare chapter with the Ikebana International but a few of us carried on (and are still going strong) with Ikebana Zimbabwe.

My next teacher was Beth Mussell. She taught me all the disciplines of Ikebana and we practiced different forms every week. I completed the full curriculum with her and achieved the four certificates and the Teacher's Course 4th Grade. There are a further eight grades in the teacher's diploma. Riji is one of the highest master degrees of Sogetsu school – something I'd like to attempt one day, and I have been having advanced lessons with an excellent Riji teacher, Mary Marques . Her unique knowledge of Ikebana is one of the reasons I enjoy my Ikebana practice mornings with her. I continue to learn something new. Mary has now upgraded me to the Teacher's Course 3rd Grade certificate.

Ikebana is no longer just a hobby or a passing interest. It's a way of life for me. I hope you will be able to share my passion through my arrangements in the pages of this book.

Anita
Eishun

FOREWORDS

Congratulations, Anita, on your achievements in Ikebana. It is a source of pride for a teacher to see a student excel and have such passion for a subject like Ikebana, too. In over thirty years of teaching Ikebana there are only a handful of students who become passionate about it and it becomes a part of one's life. Ikebana is a great study for the mind and even a therapy to calm one in the stresses of day-to-day living in the 21st century! I always say it is impossible to be creative in Ikebana unless your mind is at peace.

I was fortunate to study under three great Ikebana teachers, two of whom studied with Mr Sofu Teshigahara in Tokyo, the founder of the Sogetsu School. They were Baroness Rukavena and Mrs Vivienne Pascoe. My third teacher, Mrs June Hyman, studied Sogetsu Ikebana in Australia under Mr Norman Sparnon who in turn had studied with Mr Sofu Teshigahara in Tokyo soon after the end of the Second World War.

I eagerly follow your path in the fascinating world of Sogetsu Ikebana!

Mary Marques Cho Sei Riji teacher
Sogetsu School of Ikebana

It is with great pleasure that I write this foreword to Anita's book of Sogetsu Ikebana. It was a privilege for me to work with such a dedicated and talented pupil. During our years together, we spent many happy hours engrossed in this beautiful art form and mutually gained from each other. I am confident that readers of this book will enjoy browsing these pages. My heartfelt congratulations to you, Anita!

I began studying Ikebana in the Sogetsu School in 1970. Lorraine Napier, an excellent teacher and a devoted follower of the Sogetsu discipline, introduced me to the art, and I was soon awarded the First Teacher's Certificate. Following Lorraine's retirement, study opportunities arose at workshops held by Mr Suzuki, Norman Sparnon, Vivienne Pascoe and Yvonne Panton-Jones. In 1990 I visited the Sogetsu School in Tokyo and was awarded the Komon Degree. During Mr Suzuki's last visit to South Africa he promoted me to the degree of Master Riji.

From 1981 to 2005 I ran a school of Sogetsu with enthusiastic, talented and loyal people. It is a truism that 'once you are a teacher, by your pupils you are taught'. It is thanks to this, together with the valuable teaching from the above-mentioned masters, that I was able to go on and be appointed as an honorary life member of the Sogetsu School in 1996 and receive the Sogetsu 80th anniversary commemorative honour award.

Betty Mussell
Ka Sen—Flower Fan

My passion and appreciation for flowers led me to want to understand what Ikebana was and how it was different from everything I had done and seen before. The idea of learning about Japanese flower arranging captured my imagination. I then met Mary Marques and began my first classes in August 1987. The exciting journey, meeting new people, making new friends and learning new techniques and traditions was hugely inspiring. As a group, we studied the Sogetsu School teachings and techniques, which is the more modern version of Ikebana. During this time with Mary, I achieved two teaching certficates, third and fourth. In 1988 I was nominated to be president of Ikebana International, a role I thoroughly enjoyed and held for two years.

It was during this time I began teaching Ikebana from my garage to anyone who was interested. This was when I met Anita and introduced her to Ikebana classes. These were held in the garage, and were great fun. Watching my students grow and develop their own creativity was very rewarding. Anita, your work always stood out, you were always so keen to learn more about Ikebana. You would persist on working on something till it was just right, a perfectionist! I am so proud to see how far you have gone in Ikebana and delighted you are writing a book, this is a wonderful achievement.

Yours in Ikebana.

Lyn Pozzo
Ho Tei'

Flowers are the music of
the ground, from Earth's lips
spoken without sound

EDWIN CURRAN

1 YELLOW ARUM LILY FLOWER AND LEAF (ZANTEDESCHIA AETHIOPICA)
New Zealand Flax
(Black Adder)
Japanese ceramic vase

3 PINK GARDEN ROSE
Maize tassels from the maize plant
Floral spring
Monstera deliciosa leaf

2 HELICONIA FLOWER
Brazilian pepper, red berry branch
(Florida Holly)
Schinus terebinthifolius species of
flowering plant in the cashew family
Fibre glass vase

4 PINK TRAILING GERANIUM
Palm tree green berries
Pottery vase (made by me)

5 OBEDIENT PLANT (PHYSOSTEGIA VIRGINIANA)
Palm leaves
Fibre glass vase

6 BIRD OF PARADISE
(STRELITZIA REGINAE)
Ceramic vases (in my intitals (ab))

We grow like flowers and bear desire, the odour of the human flowers

RICHARD HENRY STODDARD

8 ZINNIA ELEGANS FLOWERS
Maranta plant
Zimabwean cast iron pot used
to cook local sadza (staple diet)

7 HELICONIA FLOWERS
Hooded Dwarf Elephant
Ear plant leaves
(Alocasia Cucullata)
Glass vases

9 WILD
AFRICAN
DAISY
Pine leaves
Bark

10 UMBRELLA
TREEPLANT
OR OCTOPUS
TREE PLANT
(SCHEFFLERA
ACTINOPHYLL)
A Zimbabwean clay pot

11 AIR PLANT (TILLANDSIA)
Dried floral twigs
Zimbabwean stone vase

12 DAY LILY
(HEMEROCALLIS)
Drift wood
Gold crest conifer
Japanese ceramic vase

13 DAY LILY
(HEMEROCALLIS)
Palm berries
Japanese ceramic vase

Flowers whisper
'Beauty!' to the world, even
as they fade, wilt, fall

JIM CARREY

14 RED CARNATIONS
Scared bamboo (Nandina Domestica)
Bark
Japanese ceramic vase

15 BLETILLA STRIATA ORCHID
Tall thin glass vase

16 CLIVIA
FLOWERS
Drift wood used as container

17 EUCALYPTUS
FICIFOLIA
Japanese ceramic vase

18 WHITE BIRDS OF PARADISE (STRELITZIA NICOLAI)
Ivy (Hedera)
Zimbabwean stone vase

19 FRANGIPANI (PLUMERIA) PLANT
Bamboo container (hand-crafted by me)

20 ARUM LILY
(ZANTEDESCHIA)
Dried pussy willow
Japanese ceramic container

21 ANTHURIUM
Dried root
Foliage of Yesterday, Today,
Tomorrow plant
(Brunfelsia pauciflora)
Moon vases

173

23 BIRD OF PARADISE
(STERLITZIA)
Bamboo strips
Bamboo containers (hand-crafted by me)

24 FLAME LILY
(GLORIOSA)
Black dry pussy willow branches
Japanese ceramic vase

25 CLIVIA
FLOWERS
Drift wood
Pottery Container

26 FLAME LILY
(GLORIOSA)
Gold crest conifer
Bamboo containers
(hand-crafted by me)

27 BIRD OF
PARADISE
(STERLITZIA)
Ivy (Hedera)
Japanese Ceramic vase

28 BUSY LIZZIE
FLOWERS
(IMPATIENS
WALLERIANA)
*Bird of Paradise
(Sterlitzia)*
Drift wood
Pottery vase

177

Flowers always make people better, happier and more helpful. They are sunshine, food and medicine for the soul

LUTHER BURBANK

29 DAYLILY (HEMEROCALLIS)

Gold crest conifer
Dry pods
Japanese ceramic vase

30 ANTHURIUM
Custard apple (Annonaceae)
Tree leaves
Japanese ceramic vase

31 FLAME LILY
(GLORIOSA)
Pomegranate tree branch
Black glass vase

33 GERBERA
FLOWER
Gold crest conifer
Hypericum berries
Drift wood
Glass lantern

35 VANDA ORCHID
Custard apple tree
(Annonaceae)
Black metal vase

Flowers are restful to look at. They have neither emotions nor conflicts

SIGMUND FREUD

36 PINK ROSE (SABINE PLATTNER ROSE)

Dried twigs from
Yesterday, Today, Tomorrow plant
(Brunfelsia pauciflora)
Pottery vase

37 ORANGE CHYRSANTHEMUMS
*Ring of trumphet vine
(Campsis)
Azelea leaves
Glass vase*

38 ANTHURIUM RED FLOWERS
*Succulent euphorba
Glass vase*

40 ANTHURIUM FLOWERS
Azalea leaves
Black and white twin ceramic vases

39 LAVENDER (LAVANDULA OR LAMIACEAE)
Japanese ceramic vase

41 ORANGE ROSES
Gold crest conifer leaves
Test tubes wired in a
twig structure

42 STRELITZIA FLOWERS
Dried palm flowers
Moon vase

43 PURPLE AGAPANTHAS
Pink budded Jasmine
(Jasminum Polyanthum)
Drift wood
Blue ceramic vase

189

Flowers are a proud
assertion that a ray of
beauty out-values all the
utilities of the world

RALPH WALDO EMERSON

44 AZALEA PLANT
Black wooden vase

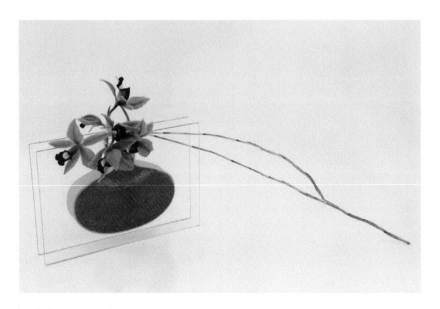

45 BLETILLA
STRIATA ORCHID
*Rectangular glass vase
with red sand*

48 PEACH GARDEN ROSE
Drift wood
Pottery vase

47 CYMBIDIUM ORCHIDS
Flax (Phormium)
Equisetum
Pottery vase

49 ARUM LILIES
(ZANTEDESCHIA)
Nandina
Wooden L-shaped vase
(designed by me)

50 POINSETTIA
(CHRISTMAS
FLOWER)
Pine
Metal cylindrical vase

52 PEACH
GARDEN ROSE
Palm berries
Zimbabwean wire vase

53 DAISY LIKE FLOWER
(CARPOBROTUS
DELICIOSUS)
Drift wood
Bamboo vase

54 CLIVIA FLOWERS
Agave attenuate
Japanese ceramic vase

55 GOLDEN TRUMPET TREE FLOWERS (TABEBUIA CHRYSOTRICHA)
Brown flax leaves
Fibre glass vase

Drift wood
Basket weave rings
Black glass vase

ACKNOWLEDGEMENTS

I would like to express my extreme gratitude to the many people who saw me through this book and to all those who provided support

My heartfelt thanks go to my mother, **Lila Kapur**, and my mother-in-law, **Ganga Bhagat**. Both excellent cooks who taught me all I know about Indian cuisine. I am eternally grateful.

Mehul & Aarti Gandhi and **Trisha Bhagat**. Thank you to my son-in-law, Mehul, for encouraging me to finish the book and for allowing me to test out recipes on him! And a huge thank you to my amazing daughters – they were the inspiration behind this book. I hope they'll continue to enjoy 'mum's cooking' throughout their lives. A special thanks to Aarti for the precise and adequate title of this book and to Trisha for designing the perfect cover.

To the men in my life, my husband, **Jayant Bhagat** and my son, **Yatish Bhagat**. Thank you for your continued support and your words of encouragement. Also, my sincere gratitude for sorting out the photography techniques. And last, but not least, for sampling all my cooked dishes and giving me a thumbs up!

An extra special thank you to **Jagu Hindocha** for dedicating his time and for his unrivalled enthusiasm and generosity regarding every aspect of the book. Your uplifting motivation assisted me through all the ups and downs from start to finish.

Thank you to my niece, **Rashmi Madan** for subbing and editing, all the copy, and for taking a genuine interest in completing and fine-tuning the book.

To my nephew, **Sanjiv Madan**, thank you for working out the best deal to design and print the book.

A big thanks to my maids, **Pinkie** and **Mhaka**, for testing out all the recipes to ensure they worked to perfection.

I'd like to also thank every single friend and family member who gave me recipes over the years! And finally, to all my Ikebana friends and teachers for sharing their beautiful arrangements and enhancing my ideas.

Anita Bhagat

This book is dedicated to my family